Preface

Like the programming language Pascal before it, the UNIX operating system has progressed from being regarded as an aberration suitable only for university and college computing, and is now recognised as an important asset to the computer professional. In some measure that reflects not only its intrinsic worth, and increasing recognition of the importance of modular systems—which UNIX unquestionably is—but also the advantages that arise from having an operating system that is largely portable between different computer systems. In this particular aspect, UNIX is the first of its generation, as FORTRAN and ALGOL were of theirs, and sets a standard against which other operating systems are compared.

Despite its early image of a highly technical system, beloved of systems fanatics and enthusiasts (and hence idealogically unsound) the UNIX operating system is well engineered and, in its seventh edition at least, is a very reliable system. This text has been written by one who can profess to be a convert to UNIX, and it is therefore to be hoped that its tone is not too unduly tainted by an excessive enthusiasm! The UNIX system is viewed here as a tool which can be used for the engineering of software; the text is not about UNIX itself, but rather tries to show how the features of UNIX can be used to help the programmer to solve problems.

Part I is necessarily tutorial in form, and introduces the UNIX system to the programmer through a gradual logical progression. Part II is unashamedly biased towards the precepts and practices that are commonly described as Software Engineering, and relates these to the ways in which we can deploy the resources of the UNIX system. Finally, Part III offers a few items of a 'how it does it' nature, in order to explain a few of the UNIX features a little more fully, largely for the benefit of the more curious reader. However, in no way does this text attempt to replace any of the system manuals!

Various people have offered advice and information at times, but I should especially like to thank Adrian King of Logica, Tony Heywood and Dominic Dunlop of Zilog, and Alan Cleary of Real Time Systems for their guidance and advice on the XENIX, ZEUS and Idris operating systems, as described in Chapter 8. I must also thank my colleagues Chic Rattray and Colin Scott who patiently read and commented on my manuscript, and even provided me with some of the examples.

This also seems a fit point at which to thank the typist, my eight fingers and right thumb for their diligent typing efforts; and my trusty Imperial 66 typewriter—a solidly engineered example of an earlier Information Technology, and one which systems such as UNIX may yet turn into the 20th century equivalent of the quill pen!

D Budgen
1984

Contents

1
Introduction

1.1 Some good intentions

It is perhaps rather hazardous to begin a text such as this by stating the aims that were in mind when it was first planned, since this opens so many opportunities for being taken to task on the many shortfalls that it is bound to contain. However, since this text has been written to try to meet what is believed to be a very real need, it is worth stating at this point just what it is that the book is attempting to achieve.

The increasing use of UNIX and the many closely related operating systems, on a variety of processors and for a wide variety of purposes, has created a whole new community of UNIX users. These new users often differ in various ways from the earlier generations of UNIX enthusiasts and may particularly differ in the amount of computer-related background that they possess. For many users, UNIX is simply a programming tool which is used to aid some particular part of their work, which might be physics, biology, engineering, commerce, etc., rather than a way of life. This text is intended to help such users, by showing how the versatility and power of UNIX can be most effectively used to meet their requirements.

Historically UNIX has been something of a 'professional' operating system, and this has particularly been reflected in the style and forms of documentation available. Faced with a system that was defended by clouds of mysterious and obscure jargon, remember that jargon = 'someone else's technical terms'!, mere mortals have sometimes been wary of UNIX. This text tries to penetrate these mists of terminology and to bring UNIX within easier reach of users whose interests lie outside pure computer science.

There is good reason for taking such a look at UNIX and encouraging non-specialists to make use of it in their work. Its original development (on PDP-7 and PDP-9 processors) was by Ken Thompson, of Bell Laboratories, whose intention was to provide himself with an operating system that possessed the facilities that he needed for software development. So the roots of the UNIX system lie in meeting a user's needs, rather than in trying to write a new and 'better' operating system as an object in itself. Much of the success of UNIX (and it is now widely regarded as the 'standard' operating system for 16-bit machines), arises from this feature of its history; the original work being later expanded in collaboration with Dennis Ritchie to produce the UNIX Operating System in more or less the form that we now know it. It is important to stress at the start that UNIX was always seen as a software tool, and so if the philosophies and methods of software engineering can be seen behind the subsequent chapters, this is not without good reason.

To assist with this aim of guiding the non-specialist reader, the text is subdivided into three main parts (subdivision of one's problems into three parts has a sound literary precedent [1]). Part I is a tutorial introduction to UNIX and the use of the principal utility programs. It describes the steps and the tools needed to build and use programs on the system, attempting at the same time to guide the reader through the maze of oddly-named utility programs (some, though not all, of the oddness may soon disappear). Inevitably it cannot be a complete or definitive guide, but the main features and facilities are described, together with simple examples where suitable.

Part II is much more concerned with actually making use of these UNIX features and concentrates on showing how conveniently some common practical requirements can be met by using them. The theme is very much one of 'UNIX as a problem-solving tool' and the examples are chosen to illustrate this aspect. This part is based around the ideas and methods of software engineering since these are practices for which UNIX offers excellent scope and support. It is in Part II that the real differences between UNIX and other operating systems really begin to show.

Part III is much shorter than the other two, and develops a little further some of the technical points, giving rather more detail than was appropriate in the earlier chapters. Although the text is really concerned with the use of UNIX, rather than with how it does things 'behind the scenes', some users may need rather more detail in some particular areas. This part is intended to help satisfy this need, the topics being chosen on the basis of the more likely developments to be contemplated by the more ambitious user.

To complete this introductory section, one limitation of the book should be clearly noted. UNIX has been implemented on a number of different makes and models of computer, becoming in many ways something of a 'benchmark' system for 16-bit and 32-bit computers. This text is based upon the widely used seventh edition of UNIX (V7). and its implementation upon the PDP-11 family of processors. While much of the material should be applicable to any processor, and almost any related system, there may well be some references that are specific to the PDP-11.

1.2   The history and philosophy of UNIX

The UNIX operating system was developed because one man wanted to be able to work with a better and more flexible operating system than those immediately available to him, and had the experience of using one (MULTICS) which possessed many desirable features.

It is therefore slightly ironic that so significant a software tool was itself more or less originated as a one-man (later two-man) exercise, rather than at the centre of some great team project! However, it is origins that are being described, and the seventh edition of UNIX has obviously passed through a considerable amount of engineering effort in the hands of a skilled team.

UNIX is sometimes considered as an operating system which is designed around a file handling system. Its file structure is very much a fundamental feature supporting many of its best points, and in particular it does embody what are generally seen to be the major virtues of UNIX—namely simplicity of structure and flexibility of use. UNIX files are regarded simply as being strings of bytes, with the programs imposing structure upon them rather than having the file handling protocols dictate how the user's programs must handle their data.

A feature of UNIX that is immediately noticeable as being different is the degree to which text processing facilities are regarded as an integral part of the UNIX toolset. Various programs of the *roff* family can be used to drive a range of printing devices and to aid in the formatting of textual output. That text processing should not be special in any way was a design aim, and it has provided UNIX with the great advantage that any programming or processing performed on UNIX can be directly supported by having its documentation stored alongside on the same file system.

A philosophy that has been a constraint upon UNIX from the beginning is that of having one software tool to do one job, i.e. that each program forming a part of UNIX should be designed to do one job, and do it well, rather than doing many jobs, some of which may not even be logically well related. As an example, UNIX uses one program to list out the contents of a directory, another to list out the contents of a file, and yet another to copy the contents of one file to another, whereas on many other systems these tasks might all be sub-tasks or **options** of one large utility program.

The UNIX approach means that the user has to remember the names of more system programs than may be necessary on some other operating systems, although the subset of frequently used programs is rarely very large. However, there is no more difficulty in that than in remembering which of the option-selecting 'switches' needs to be used to direct a multi-purpose program to the required task.

The real power that can be the reward of this approach only begins to emerge fully when in a later chapter we come to look at **shell programming**. By means of shell programs we are easily able to 'plumb together' a number of such single-task programs to produce more specialist programs. (The term 'plumb' is consistent with such terms as 'pipe' and 'tee', which we will encounter later in this context.) With these methods the user can easily create a varied range of programs by combining a series of tested and tried programs, thereby also reducing the debugging time that would be needed if more conventional programming methods were used. So 'modular' techniques are nothing new to UNIX!

For the moment though, further discussion of such ideas resembles attempts to run before having mastered walking, and descriptions of other UNIX features will be deferred to the end of Part I.

1.3   Variations from standard UNIX

UNIX is distributed to licensed user sites in both binary and source forms, so leaving users free to make significant changes to the system should they choose to do so, depending on available skills and needs. Inevitably, different sites have utilised this freedom to different degrees, leading to a number of different local options, some being more widely adopted than others. (The situation is rather similar to the way in which each computer manufacturer has tended to produce their own variants on standard FORTRAN—some extensions having become almost *de facto* standards, others being much more machine or system-specific. The comparison with FORTRAN is one that is often made, since UNIX has liberated operating systems from machine-dependence in much the same way that FORTRAN earlier liberated programming from dependence on a particular machine instruction set.)

As a result, many computer installations have features or utility programs that do not exactly tally with those described in this text. Differences should usually be minor, and can be solved by adding margin notes if necessary, but at this point it is worth mentioning two areas where differences are particularly likely to be found and may be a little more marked.

The first of these is the way in which the terminal handler program handles the characters typed in at a user's terminal. This program is used by the system to control the terminal's operation (the terminal may be a visual display unit or a hard-copy printing terminal), and to provide facilities to aid the user in using the system. On occasion we may wish to direct the terminal handler to do something other than just receive or output lines of characters, such as to forget the last character typed in (to **delete** it), or temporarily to freeze the output of characters to our screen. To issue these instructions, we usually type in special non-printing codes, selected by using the terminal's **control** key as a 'shift'. For historical reasons the original Bell Laboratories version of the program has some slightly unconventional choices for the codes that select some of these control functions, and other versions have become quite widely used. In Chapter 3, where we describe how to interact with UNIX, the variant of terminal handler program described is one that is currently in use in many sites within the UK; this is not the original Bell version. The reader should find relatively little difficulty in using either version, and where appropriate the forms used by the Bell Laboratories version are also given.

The second feature where variations are frequently to be found concerns text editing. The standard UNIX interactive text editor program, *ed*, is not particularly conversational or helpful ('curt' might describe it more aptly), and it is oriented towards line editing. So a variety of text editors have become available, many of them able to exploit the features of the versatile visual display units now available. Since *ed* is still likely to be available alongside these editors, and the variations are much too wide to be adequately covered in a text such as this, Chapter 5, which deals with text editing, has been limited to describing how to get started using *ed*.

Apart from these two features and another which is described in the next section, no attempt has been made to catalogue or describe the many variations on the theme of UNIX V7 that have inevitably been produced by so skilled and idiosyncratic a community as the UNIX users.

1.4   Other systems and 'look-alikes'

Bell Laboratories, who were the originators of UNIX, were at first unable to market and support UNIX commercially because of legal technicalities, and so the use of UNIX was largely confined to use within their own extensive organisation and licensed sites within the academic community. The latter were prepared to accept it with no backup or support in exchange for the facilities that it offered, and were able to provide enough in-house expertise to manage their own support and maintenance, as well as being able to pool knowledge with other users.

The evident benefits of UNIX then led to a variety of UNIX versions and 'look-alikes' (similar externally, but different internally) becoming available to a wider range of computer users. These were produced by software houses who were not bound by the same legal knots as Bell Laboratories, and who could market such systems with the provision for backup and support that the commercial user generally requires.

While a survey of the many operating systems that can be gathered together under this heading is beyond an introductory work such as this, three examples of such systems have been outlined in Chapter 8. The chapter illustrates the main forms in which these examples differ from UNIX V7, and what significant enhancements have been incorporated in them. For many of the available systems the differences are slight enough for this text to serve as a practical introduction to their use too.

1.5   Teaching aids on UNIX

If Part I of this book can be regarded as some form of UNIX primer, there is still a need to practise the skills described, and some aid for the new user is available from UNIX itself. Two particular programs are worth noting under this heading.

The first is connected with text handling facilities, which are a particularly strong feature of UNIX. The UNIX manuals are themselves maintained and printed using these facilities; and since the manuals can be stored in the filestore, the appropriate text processing programs can be directed to route the output to a user's screen instead of to a printing device. A utility program, *man* (short for *man*ual) has been provided for this purpose, providing most of the aid that might be expected from a 'help' facility by printing the appropriate information to the user's screen on request.

As an example of the use of *man*, suppose we want to find out more about the program *ls*, which is used to provide a list of the files that we possess (more about this soon). We enter the command

```
$ man 1 ls
```

(Note that the '$' already appears as our prompt from the system.) The '1' indicates that the appropriate volume of the manuals is Volume 1, since we only want a summary of the features of *ls*, and the 'ls' tells *man* which entry we want. The *man* program will then output the appropriate entry from the manual to our screen.

A second program, of a rather different sort, is *learn*. This program can provide interactive tutorial sessions on a variety of UNIX features including file handling, the text editor and even the C compiler. It works through a set of graduated examples—and marks your exercises too! Since it is self explanatory in use, a useful way to follow up a reading of Part I of this book might be to sit down at a terminal, log on to the system and type the command

```
$ learn
```

Good luck!

1.6   Textual conventions

To provide some clarity in presenting so technical a topic, a few simple layout conventions have been maintained throughout this text.

The first is that the name of any UNIX process (or **program** if you prefer—the difference is explained in Chapter 2) occurring in the text is printed in italics. We have already met examples of this convention when referring to the utility for printing out the manual, *man*, the text editor, *ed*, and the *learn* program.

A second convention, used as sparingly as possible, is to indicate any items that can be reasonably omitted on a first reading. Where this applies to a whole section, the section heading is marked with an asterisk (*); where it is material within a section it is placed between square brackets, as in

```
[ ...... ]
```

While these items are relevant to a full tutorial coverage, many new users may not immediately need the depth of detail included in these sections. So while the more experienced user may be happy to include them on a first reading, they can be safely omitted by those who feel that they already have quite enough information to absorb.

As a third convention, where command lines have optional parameter fields associated with them, these have been denoted by enclosing the optional part in braces, as in the command

```
$ cat file1 { file2 file3 ... filen }
```

which implies that only the name of 'file1' must always be specified, though more filenames may be given if the user wishes.

The last point is not strictly a convention, but is very important and concerns the possible ambiguity of printed characters. In most typefaces (especially those commonly used on computer terminals), there is considerable similarity between the lower-case letter 'l' and the numeral '1'. The UNIX literature widely uses lower-case letters, and this book follows that pattern. Although UNIX does differentiate between upper- and lower-case characters, it can cope with terminals that only support upper-case characters. Confusion between these two characters can easily arise, leading to unexpected error messages and odd effects when trying to run programs or select options.

For the tutorial Chapters (Part I), each chapter has been prefaced by a short list of keywords, which summarise the concepts and terms presented within it. Where appropriate, there are also references for further reading quoted at the end of a chapter. Those described only by title and author are from the UNIX V7 manual.

Reference

1.   *The Gallic Wars.* Caesar, J, (various publishers).

Part I

2
Where to begin

Keywords

shell; process; a.out

2.1 Introduction

Any programmer who is setting out to use a particular operating system for the first time will need to learn some basic points about its use before being able to perform even the most simple tasks with it. A more experienced programmer does have the advantage though of being able to draw upon previous learning experiences, and existing knowledge, to help him select the information about the system that is likely to be most immediately useful. This is a significant advantage over a less experienced programmer, since the relevant information may only be available in the form of less than readable reference manuals, possibly spread over several volumes, requiring some programming experience in order to be able to sift for the information required.

This chapter attempts to provide the benefits of experience to help the new user in coming to grips with the UNIX operating system. It begins by establishing a list of the basic skills that a new user will most need to acquire, and then goes on to show how the remainder of Part I helps in meeting these needs in a well-ordered sequence.

2.2 The new user's needs

What basic set of user skills can be established as being really essential for the user who is encountering UNIX for the first time? These can most readily be determined by first considering which common tasks a user is likely to want to tackle with UNIX, and then determining which practical skills are needed to manage these. Some common tasks are likely to include:

(i)   to be able to communicate with UNIX, i.e. to know how to pass commands to the system, and to know what commands must be used in order to obtain the effects or information needed;
(ii) to be able to develop new programs (and modify existing ones), and therefore to know how to use a basic group of the **utility programs** that are provided with the system for this purpose;
(iii) to be able to use such programs; this requires the ability to input data to the program and to obtain meaningful output from it.

The performance of each of these tasks will require some knowledge about a number of UNIX features and facilities. However, as will be seen, it is possible to perform a wide variety of tasks on UNIX using only a fairly small vocabulary of commands and with a working knowledge of only a few of the many utility programs; though to make really effective use of UNIX we then need to build upon this knowledge.

In summary, the new user needs to be able to perform the following set of basic tasks:

> communicate
> develop programs
> run programs

and the next subsections will show how the rest of Part I helps the user to set about these tasks.

2.2.1   Communicating with UNIX

This is the first and most fundamental task, since until the basics of this have been mastered we cannot perform any useful work.

The first task in communicating is to be able to **log on**, i.e. to identify ourselves to UNIX, verifying our identity by means of a **password**. UNIX will then accept our commands as being suitably authorised.

Once this has been done, UNIX uses a program called the *shell* to interpret our commands and requests as they are typed in at the keyboard of our terminal. The *shell* is roughly equivalent to the **command interpreter** or **console monitor** of other operating systems. As a user we do not need to know anything about how the *shell* works, only to know what formats should be used for commands and the sort of responses that we should expect to get to those commands. The *shell* can be used in simple and straightforward fashion, although it is also capable of providing some very powerful facilities.

The basic task of communicating with UNIX therefore identifies two particular needs for a user, namely

> to send commands to UNIX

and

> to interpret its responses

Chapter 3 is concerned with how to use the *shell* and includes sufficient detail to allow a reader to be able to progress through the tasks covered in the rest of Part I. Some of the more versatile features of the *shell* are covered in Chapter 7, where the difference between UNIX and other operating systems begins to be more clearly apparent.

2.2.2   Developing new programs

An operating system such as UNIX is mainly used to develop new programs or to modify existing ones. These programs might be written in one or more of a wide variety of programming languages, from the low level of assembler code up to powerful languages such as Prolog, Pascal, Modula-2 or Ada. Regardless of the programming language used, there are a number of basic tasks that must be performed when developing a program. These are fairly sequential in nature, and can be summarised as follows:

(a)   creating or modifying a file of text (the **source code**), i.e. the file containing, say, our FORTRAN or Pascal program;

(b)   translating (compiling) this source file in order to produce a file which contains some form of intermediate code, or **object code**, more closely related to the machine language of the computer;

(c)   link-editing (or **linking**) this new object file with the **library routines** and possibly with other independently or separately compiled object files to produce the final **executable** program file which can be **run** under the control of the operating system. (This stage is not involved for interpreted languages such as BASIC or Prolog.)

(For many of the high-level languages that are available on UNIX, as well as for the assembler, the UNIX system will combine stages (b) and (c) unless it is explicitly commanded not to do so. So for much of the time, the existence of a separate pass (c) can conveniently be forgotten.)

File creation and modification
The first step in the suggested development sequence assumes that the source code for the program will not only be created, but will also be modified. This reflects the fact that a new program will rarely (or never!) compile and run successfully the first time through the system. This implies that the sequence of tasks:

> (a) – (b) – (c)

forms the core of a loop (or, more accurately, of two loops), and that these loops are likely to be repeated a number of times before the program can be deemed to be completed and working. So a user will also need some knowledge about how to perform some simple **housekeeping** of the various files. This will include performing such tasks as:

> creating text files;
> performing simple editing of text files;
> obtaining a list of the files currently owned by the user;
> deleting unwanted files.

This is a very basic set of actions and most users will soon need additional facilities, chiefly to perform further tasks such as:

> renaming files;
> grouping files together in some way;
> archiving copies of files;
> changing a file's **protection**, to prevent accidental erasure of the file or access to it
>   by unauthorised users.

To get started on these tasks, Chapter 4 looks at how files are used and managed on the UNIX system, what naming conventions are supported and how a user can perform most of the functions outlined above. Chapter 5 completes the introduction to file handling by detailing the ways to create and modify files using *ed*, the standard UNIX text editor program.

Compiling and link-editing
Having entered the source code into a file, the next stage in program development is usually to try to compile the file and, if this is successful, to link-edit the resultant object code with the support library routines in order to produce an executable program.

Historically UNIX has provided its most extensive forms of support for the programming language C, in the shape of library routines and associated utility programs. C is a language which can be regarded either as a 'high-level assembler', or as a concise form of 'structured language' for system programming, according to your preferences and prejudices! It is a powerful language which was primarily designed for the purpose of building the UNIX operating system itself, as well as for writing the supporting software tools (**utility programs**).

The other language well supported on UNIX is the long-established language FORTRAN. UNIX can even claim to have had the first widely available compiler for the FORTRAN 77 standard, though inevitably with some extensions to the standard too.

Compilers have been produced by various groups for many other languages, and provided that your taste in languages is not too obscure, then there is likely to be a compiler lurking somewhere (and if not, then there are some powerful software tools to help you build your own). Indeed, if the language is popular enough (e.g. Pascal), then there may be a multiplicity of compilers available.

The link-editing stage is generally well concealed from the user, and nearly all of the available compilers will automatically run the link-editor if a compilation pass is successful, unless explicitly directed otherwise. However, its presence is occasionally revealed by the error messages that it produces, and so it cannot be wholly overlooked even in an introductory text such as this.

A user's requirements for the compilation stages will partly depend upon the chosen programming language and so Chapter 6 describes how programs can be compiled and linked using the C or FORTRAN compilers, these being the most widely available; FORTRAN is also the most widely known of the languages supported on UNIX. There is also a short introduction to the use of the assembler.

2.2.3 Running a program

Once all of the hurdles of construction have finally been overcome, and a program has been successfully compiled and linked with its support routines, then we need to be able to use it. UNIX documentation usually refers to the file produced by the link-editor as an **executable** program file, and when such a file is copied into the computer's memory and run under the control of the operating system then it forms what is known as a **process**. By convention, the UNIX link-editor will normally write the executable program image it produces into a file named 'a.out'; and so in the UNIX literature this name is sometimes used as a general term to describe all such executable files.

To do any useful work the running process also needs to be able to receive input(s) of data and/or commands, and to produce meaningful outputs. When not using the terminal keyboard and screen for input and output, the user must identify to the system where it will find the appropriate files of input data and where to create new output files to receive the results of a 'run'.

The first part of Chapter 7 covers the basic steps that are involved in running programs and explains how a user can specify the input and output files and devices to be used. It also gives a short description of some of the software tools and methods that can be used to **debug** a process which fails to execute in the intended manner. The latter part of the chapter then shows how the full facilities of the UNIX *shell* can be used to help in creating and using our programs; and shows how the UNIX philosophy of 'one job—one program' can be coupled with these to produce the UNIX 'flavour'.

2.3 Variants

Chapter 8 is the last chapter in Part I, and gives a short introduction to three examples taken from the expanding selection of UNIX-like operating systems. Within fairly narrow limits, this chapter tries to indicate particular areas of usage where such systems may differ in their functions and facilities from those described in the rest of Part I.

2.4 Summary

This chapter has shown that by identifying a set of tasks that the user will usually need to perform, namely:

> communication with UNIX
> developing programs
> running programs

it is possible to produce a list of the skills that are needed to perform these tasks and hence to provide an orderly introduction to the system for the new user. Table 2.1 provides a summary of the suggested needs that accompany each task and indicates which of the chapters of Part I can provide the means of meeting each need.

Table 2.1 Summary of user tasks and needs

Task	Need	Appropriate chapter
Communicate	Send commands.	Chapter 3
	Interpret UNIX responses.	Chapter 3
Develop or modify programs	Create text files.	Chapter 5
	Edit text files.	Chapter 5
	List files owned by user.	Chapter 4
	Delete unwanted files.	Chapter 4
	Rename files.	Chapter 4
	Group/archive files.	Chapter 4
	Protect files.	Chapter 4
	Compile source files.	Chapter 6
	Link-edit files.	Chapter 6
Run a program	Select inputs and outputs.	Chapter 7
	'Debug' run-time errors.	Chapter 7

3
Getting started

Keywords

shift; control; password; *ls*; *cat*; *rm*; *cp*; *mv*; *grep*; *passwd*; metacharacter; prompt; option;. profile

3.1 Some conventions

Since this chapter is mainly concerned with establishing communication between a user and UNIX, it may be useful to begin it with a brief review of a few terms that will be used. Most of these terms may already be familiar.

UNIX can support a variety of models and types of terminal, some being hard copy devices such as teletypes and serial printers, while the others are usually VDUs (visual display units) using a television-type screen. All types of terminal will normally have a conventional layout of the main keys on the keyboard (often referred to as a QWERTY layout) and in order to be able to do anything at all, users must at least be able to find the appropriate keys on their particular keyboard! We will use this keyboard to send our commands to UNIX, and for consistency of terminology will assume that the echoes of such inputs and any replies or other output text are received on a screen, although on a hard copy terminal the outputs will actually be printed on paper.

Computer terminals usually have two distinct 'shift' keys on the keyboard, so that each normal character key can be used to perform three functions; compared with the two functions of conventional typewriter keys (upper- and lower-case characters). The key that is marked 'shift' is essentially identical in purpose with the shift key of a typewriter, and if it is held down while a character key is pressed, the upper-case form of the character will be entered. On a terminal which can print upper-case characters only, such as an UPPER-CASE ONLY VDU or a teletype, the 'shift' key will have no effect when used with the alphabetical character keys, and will only affect the numeric block along the top row of the keyboard. For the purposes of this text we will generally assume that a user's terminal does have lower-case printing available, as most of the UNIX documents assume this in their examples.

The second key of this type is usually marked 'control', or an abbreviation of that such as ctrl, and is used to generate an extra set of functions from the character keys of the keyboard. When the control key is held down and a character key is pressed, the resultant code generated is referred to as a **control character.** Control characters are non-printing characters, in that a code is generated and sent to the computer but the code does not correspond to any of the normal printing characters and so is not echoed on the screen. A small set of control characters are widely used when communicating with the system.

In this text we will differentiate between upper- and lower-case characters in the normal way—by printing them as such. For example, a A; b B; c C

We will refer to the non-printing codes generated by holding down the control key and pressing a character key as 'control-char', where 'char' is any normal printing character. For example,

control-A

So to type 'control-U' simply means the act of holding down the control key with one finger and pressing the U key with another. Note that when referring to the 'control' shift we do not need to differentiate between upper- and lower-case characters.

On terminals which are capable of reproducing both lower- and upper-case characters, there may also be a key marked 'TTY CAPS' or similar. This is a key which may be locked in down position to change all alphabetical characters to upper-case, still leaving the 'shift' key to operate as normal on the remaining characters of the keyboard. This effectively turns the terminal into one which can handle upper-case characters only.

Finally, when using the UNIX *shell*, the spaces which separate the different parts of a command line are significant, and are recognised by the *shell* as being the separators of the parts or **fields** of the command. The examples have not used any special symbols to emphasise this point, but do remember when typing in commands for yourself that the spaces do matter.

3.2   Logging on to UNIX

Before continuing, the reader should note that the conventions described here as being used for some of the functions ('delete' etc.) are not those that are used by the standard Bell Laboratories version of the terminal handler and described as such in their manuals, but instead are those used widely in UK installations of UNIX. This is unfortunately an area where a number of variants are in use, and the user may need to make a note of local forms.

The first action when using almost any operating system is to **log on**, and to identify ourselves to the system by this act, so that it knows who we are and therefore what privileges of access we may have to various items of information.

Before we can log on for the first time, we need to acquire some form of **user identifier**, which will be allocated to us in the form of a unique character string, and which will also have been declared to the operating system. The form that our identifier will take will depend upon local practice; it may be our first name, our surname, initials, or some other code (to the operating system it is just a string of characters anyway). For the examples in the rest of this chapter we shall assume that we have been given the user identifier of 'NewUser', and that this has been declared to the system and is ready for us to use.

Our terminal will usually be displaying the prompt

login:

and, if not, this can usually be obtained by pressing the 'return' (or 'newline') key. We can then identify ourselves by typing our name 'NewUser', followed by pressing the 'return' key. (Unless indicated otherwise, all lines of input should be terminated by pressing the 'return' key and this will not be explicitly shown in the examples.) So we now have the line

```
login: NewUser
```

on our screen.

If our terminal can handle upper-case characters only, then we need to indicate in some way that the letters 'N' and 'U' are in upper-case (since the system will normally convert all characters from such a terminal to lower-case for internal use). We do this by typing the special character '\' before any letter that needs to be kept as upper-case, so getting the rather messy line

```
login: \NEW\USER
```

which will then be stored internally as 'NewUser'.

Once we have declared our identity in this way, UNIX will respond by checking that we really are who we are claiming to be. It does this by asking us for our password, requesting this via the prompt:

```
password:
```

on the next line. Again, when using the system for the first time it will depend on local convention as to what the password will be. If no password has been allocated then we indicate the absence of a password by just pressing the 'return' key; UNIX will check in this case that no password is expected. For some variants of the terminal handler, no 'password:' prompt will be issued if no password has been set for an identifier.

If a password has been allocated, or when logging on after setting one ourselves (see p. 24), this must be typed in and terminated with the usual 'return'. However, providing that the terminal is running using normal full duplex transmission, there will be no echo on the screen as the characters of the password are typed in. The echo is suppressed at this point so that other users cannot casually obtain your password by seeing your screen or print-out. For an upper-case terminal, the '\' character must again be used to indicate any upper-case letters in the password.

If UNIX is not satisfied that we have adequately established our credentials, usually because we will have mis-typed our user identifier or password, then it will simply prompt again via the prompt

```
login:
```

and we can have another try! Once UNIX is satisfied as to our identity then it will invoke the *shell* process to handle our commands, and our terminal session can begin.

3.3 Conversing with the *shell*

When a copy of the *shell* is started up to handle the requests and commands that we issue through our terminal, it begins by performing a number of tasks of a housekeeping nature and, depending on local organisation, will print out on our screen the contents of a text file used to hold the 'message of the day', etc. This is the standard means for passing on news and information to users.

When these tasks are complete, the *shell* will then prompt us and await our commands. The usual prompt is the character '$'. (This can be easily changed if we prefer something different, as will be shown later.)

On the whole, the UNIX *shell* is rather non-conversational. It listens to what we say via our keyboard, but gives very little indication of what it thinks of our commands in terms of any lengthy error messages or warnings. In some cases, when we do make an error in our command, it may even ignore it and just prompt again—so it may pay to check the results of each action while finding our way around the system. UNIX is a good listener, but rather impassive about it!

Once we have obtained a prompt from the *shell*, we can proceed to give some commands to it. These are typed in as usual, terminating each command line by pressing the 'return' key. UNIX will then perform the requested action before prompting us again. As an example, to check which files are currently in our directory we can type 'ls', as in

        $ ls

Of course, the '$' is already there. The program *ls* will then list out the names of any files that we currently own. (Note that there is no 'run' command; if the name of an executable program is typed in, then the program will be copied into the computer's memory and executed by the *shell* as a process.)

3.3.1 Correcting typing errors

Inevitably we will make some mistakes when typing in our command lines, so it is useful to know how these can be corrected, assuming that they are noticed before we have pressed the 'return' key. If we type a wrong character while entering a line, then the effect of the last character typed can be erased by pressing the 'delete' (or 'rubout') key, and repeated pressing of this key will erase backwards through the string already input, one character at a time. (On a VDU this usually erases the characters from the screen; on a hard-copy terminal they will be echoed again as they are erased from the buffer, and usually delimited by the character pair '[]'.) For example, if when using a hard-copy terminal we accidentally type the line

        $ pascla

and realise our mistake, then we can press the 'delete' key twice to get

        $ pascla[al

and then type 'al' to produce the final line

        $ pascla[al]al

This will have the same effect as if we had originally typed correctly

        $ pascal

Note that on the standard Bell Laboratories terminal handler, the 'delete' function is performed by pressing the '#' key.

If the mistake has occurred near the beginning of a long line of text, and has not been noticed for some time, it may be easier to clear the whole line from the terminal handler's buffer. This can be done by pressing control-U (remember, hold 'control' down and press 'U'). This removes the whole line from the buffer and hence UNIX ignores everything that has been typed since the previous 'return'. With a VDU the whole line may be erased from the screen too; otherwise the handler may just echo a new line character and there will be no indication on the print-out that the line was abandoned. On the original Bell Laboratories version this is achieved by pressing the '@' character.

The ability to make corrections in this way is made possible because of the special terminal handling process, which controls the reading of the keyboard and the output of characters to the screen. This does not pass on a line of characters until the 'return' key is pressed. Even if a program reads its input on a character-by-character basis, the whole line will first be read in to the terminal handler's buffer, and only after 'return' has been pressed will the terminal handler pass the line, one character at a time, to the program. The advantage of this system is that a user's program does not need to consider or handle such messy features as the 'delete' and control-U functions for themselves, these services being provided by the terminal handling process.

One other useful control character to remember is control-C. This has the effect of causing the *shell* to abandon the current running process (essentially, all processes run under the supervision of the *shell* process). It may be useful on such occasions as when a running process is producing lots of unwanted output, perhaps because there has been a programming error, or because the wrong data has been used as the input. Typing control-C will cause the process to be abandoned and in this case will stop the flow of text to the screen. On the original Bell Laboratories version, this function is performed by pressing the 'delete' key.

3.3.2   Controlling output

On some occasions, especially when using the utility *cat* to list the contents of a file, or when listing the contents of the text editor's buffer, we may generate a listing that is too long for the whole of it to fit on to our screen at once. To prevent information flashing past our eyes and being lost, some simple paging control is provided by the terminal handling process.

Normally control-S will suspend print-out, and depending on implementation, control-Q will resume it again. (For the Bell Laboratories version, another control-S performs the release.) The version of the terminal handler commonly used in the UK will normally limit output to one screenfull at a time, and the user must actively request the next line by pressing 'return', or the next full screen by pressing any other character key (usually the 'space' bar).

Table 3.1 summarises the special characters that control these basic functions. A few of the printing characters are also used to perform special tasks, and these 'metacharacters' will be described more fully later.

3.4   Using the utility programs

We have already seen some examples of how to direct the *shell* to execute a program, which is simply to type in its name or, more correctly, the name of the file in which the appropriate program is stored. For example;

```
$ ls
```

Most UNIX utility programs (i.e. the set of programs that are supplied as a part of the operating system) tend to have rather brief names that do not immediately reflect their purpose. The directory listing utility that was used above, *ls*, stands for 'list directory'— and others are even less obviously named!

Many of these programs, including *ls*, simply output information and do not expect to be given any further input from us while they are running. A few, most notably the

Table 3.1   A summary of useful terminal control functions. The equivalent characters for the Bell Laboratories terminal handler are given in parentheses.

Key	Operation performed
delete (#)	Erases the last character that was typed in. (Sometimes marked as 'rubout'.)
control-U (@)	Erases the current line just typed in.
control-C (delete)	Aborts the current running process (unless this is the *shell*).
return	Terminates the current line of input and will be recognised by the terminal handler process which will then pass the line on to the appropriate receiving process. (Sometimes marked 'newline'.)
space	Separates the fields of a command. ('Tab' will do the same.)
control-Z (control-D)	Terminates the *shell* process and hence ends the current interactive session.
control-S	Used to suspend output to the screen. Restarted by control-Q (control-S).

interactive text editor program, do expect further inputs from us in order to perform their functions. Sometimes such programs do not give any further prompts to the user to indicate that input is needed—a rather confusing feature. However, some programs use a **secondary prompt** character, which is the character '>'. This has been chosen to be different from the **primary prompt** of the *shell* ($) for the obvious reasons of making clearer to the user that the request is being produced by the utility.

A few simple, but very powerful, utility programs that a new user should quickly become acquainted with, together with their functions, are as follows:

ls   to list directory contents, i.e. filenames;
cat   to copy the contents of one or more files to the terminal screen;
rm   to remove (delete) the named file(s);
cp   to copy one file into another;
mv   to move a file to another directory and/or rename it (note that unlike *cp* the original identity is lost);
grep to search the selected file(s) in order to match a given string of characters and print out each occurrence of a match that it finds.

A mistake made when typing in the name of a program that we wish to run will generate one of the few error messages that the UNIX *shell* ever produces. For example, if we type

```
$ lx
```

instead of the correct name

```
$ ls
```

then the *shell* will be unable to find a file named 'lx' in the appropriate directories and will print out the (typically terse) message:

```
lx: not found
```

and then prompt again for input.

3.4.1   Using our own programs

Our own executable programs are executed in just the same manner as we use when running utility programs, i.e. by typing in the name of the file that contains the program. As an example, if we have compiled a program into the standard file 'a.out', then to run this we just type in

```
$ a.out
```

The *shell* will first search our own directory for any file that we name in this way, executing the program in it, if found. Should it fail to find the file (perhaps because it is a utility program that we are requesting), then it proceeds to search two other directories in which utility programs are stored. Should it still fail to find the file then the *shell* will print out the '<file>: not found' message. The order in which the directories are searched is known as the **search path**; and this being UNIX, the default search path can of course be changed by the user if required.

We should avoid identifying our files by such names as 'ls' or 'cat' that are already in use on the system. If we do so then when we want a standard utility the *shell* will try to execute our files instead, because our files are encountered earlier on the search path.

3.4.2   Selecting options

The UNIX utility programs usually perform only one task, in accordance with the UNIX philosophy of one program to perform one job. However, they do require some inputs from us in order to do their work. The utility *rm* will require the names of any files that it is to delete (the full specification of filenames is covered in Chapter 4), while *grep* needs the file name(s) and also the string of characters which is to be used as the pattern to be matched.

The usual method of specifying any input **parameters**, i.e. filenames or patterns, is to enter them on the same line as the program name, separated by spaces. For example,

```
$ rm myfile
```

causes *rm* to delete the file named 'myfile'.

Even with the UNIX philosophy of one program for one task, we may still need to select between optional forms of input and output, and possibly other forms of action. So we will need to be able to pass our choice to the program by selecting **options** (or 'switches' as they are sometimes known on other systems), when the program is run. These are normally entered on the same line as the program name, and parameters and are usually (but not always) preceded by the character '–' to distinguish them from the parameters. Being UNIX, the options for most utility programs are selected via single letters.

If we take the example of *ls* again, then there are several options that we can select, although we are not likely to need most of them at this point. If we choose none and just type the command

```
$ ls
```

then we will get a simple list of the names of the files in our directory in alphabetical order, one name to a line. For example,

```
$ ls
one
three
two
$
```

will indicate that we own the files named 'one', 'two' and 'three'. The use of the option '–l', as in

```
$ls -1
```

will give the same list, but now adding further information about each file. For each file we are now informed about who may access it (see Chapter 4), the user identifier of the owner of the file (usually ourselves), the size of the file in bytes, and the date and time at which the file was last modified in any way. For the above example, this may now look something like

```
$ ls -1
-rw-rw-r--   1  NewUser        712  March 10  11:42  one
-rw-rw-r--   1  NewUser       1232  March 12  10:21  three
-rw-rw-r--   1  NewUser        203  March 10  13:12  two
$
```

Another option for *ls* is '–t', and the command

```
$ ls -t
```

will change the ordering of the filenames from alphabetical ordering to being listed in the order of the time of last modification, with the most recently changed files first. Options can usually be combined (where this is not inconsistent) as in

```
$ ls -1t
```

which will produce a full listing of information about the files, but now ordered by the time of the last modification rather than alphabetically.

This example highlights the similarity of the letter 'l' and the numeral '1' in many typefaces. The user should always be alert to the possibility of confusing them, especially as single letter options are so widely used.

Note that when options and filenames both appear as parameters of a program, then the options must be stated before any filenames; for example

```
$ ls -1 one
```

will list in full the specifications of the file named 'one' only.

3.5 Logging out

It is only too easy to begin something that you cannot end when first learning your way around a new operating system. Typically this will occur when using interactive programs such as the text editor, or possibly the debugging tool. Unfortunately most user manuals are keener to explain how to get started with using such tools than to explain how to terminate the session, and the desperate programmer may find himself using such brute force methods of escape as the use of control-C, which may or may not succeed.

Logging out at the end of a terminal session is another such problem. For UNIX this is simplicity itself. Pressing the control-Z character will instruct the *shell* to terminate, and a new

```
login:
```

will appear on the screen. The control-Z character is commonly used to indicate the logical **end-of-file** when using the keyboard as an input to a program, and this is just what we are doing here—the *shell* being the program which is informed that there is no more input from the keyboard. (For the Bell Laboratories version of the terminal handler, the exit character is control-D instead of control-Z.)

Do remember to log out when finishing work at the terminal. If you fail to do so then the next user who comes along will have full access to all of your files, together with all of your power over them—which could be a disaster. Switching off the terminal will not help either; you will still be logged on when it is switched on again.

3.6   An example terminal session

Having described the basic features of using the UNIX system interactively, it may help to work through a simple and short example. Figure 3.1 shows the print-out generated from a simple interactive session on UNIX.

The session is simple enough. The user (identity 'NewUser') begins by logging on, but as he makes a spelling error in his identifier his first attempt is rejected and he has to try again.

Successful on this second attempt, he then gets a brief 'message of the day' from the local system manager followed by a prompt from the *shell*. NewUser then lists his directory entries to remind himself of the files that he currently owns, and then lists them again more fully to remind himself of how large they are. Finding one that has a size of 0 bytes, produced by a program error in a previous session, he deletes this file using *rm*. (Usually this occurs when the program is aborted via control-C, or terminates abnormally because of a programming error, so that the file is not properly closed.)

The user then makes a copy of another of his files (making a mistake when first typing in the command line, and needing to correct this), and finally runs the *grep* utility to find out which of his files are using a variable called 'newline' or have the string 'newline' appearing in the text. Not surprisingly, both the original and the copied files give the same result. Finally he logs off from the system. Note that the final control-Z produces no print-out, hence the last line apparently contains only a prompt character.

This short session has only used a few of the features mentioned so far, but should help by showing how they are actually used.

3.7   Passwords

A user's password is the 'doorkey' needed to gain access to the system and to his files. We can protect our files from being read by others (and ourselves), or being written to by anyone, using the methods described in Chapter 4. As the owner of a file we can always change these protections, and hence the ultimate protection for them lies in the password mechanism which enables the system to verify our identity.

As a new user you may be given a password when you are first enrolled on to the local

```
login: Newuser
password:
login: NewUser
password:

    ** line printer being serviced at 1200 **

$ ls
a.out
layers.dat
test.f
test.o
test.lst
xray.f
xray.o
$ ls -l
total 20
-rwxrwxr-x 1 NewUser          3494 Jan  8   11:29   a.out
-rw-r--r-- 1 NewUser           954 Feb 10   10:08   layers.dat
-rw-rw-r-- 1 NewUser           705 Jan  3   11:54   test.f
-rw-rw-r-- 1 NewUser          2034 Jan  3   11:58   test.o
-rw-rw-r-- 1 NewUser          1206 Jan  3   11:58   test.lst
-rw-rw-r-- 1 NewUser           466 Feb 14   13:23   xray.f
-r--r--r-- 1 NewUser             0 Feb 14   13:25   xray.o
$ rm xray.o
$ cp xra.f[f.]y.f newtest.f
$ grep newline xray.f newtest.f
newtest.f:   newline = 3
newtest.f:   do 122 i = 1, newline
xray.f:      newline = 3
xray.f:      do 122 i = 1, newline
$

login:
```

Fig. 3.1 An example terminal session on UNIX

UNIX system, or it might be left to you to set it up for yourself when you first log on. Whichever is the case, a password needs to be changed from time to time in order to increase its security, especially where there is any reason to believe that it has become known to others.

The system stores passwords in an encrypted (coded) form, and such is the power claimed for the encryption algorithm and the difficulty of reversing it that its general form is fairly well known! When, as part of the logging on process, you type in your password, this input will be encrypted in turn and compared with the stored version. Working out a password from the stored version is virtually impossible—so don't forget your password!

To ensure that the encryption mechanism can do its work effectively, a password should be at least six characters long. To avoid having a password guessed by other users it is generally sensible to avoid using such obvious possibilities as family names, road names, etc. One useful idea is to use a deliberate mis-spelling of a common word. Passwords are set by the *passwd* utility program (an easily remembered name), and *passwd* will, sensibly, ensure that you know your current password before allowing you to make any changes. If you are careless enough to forget to log out, at least no-one can come along and change your password! As *passwd* will not echo either the old or new passwords, for extra security it checks your choice of the new one by making you enter it twice.

To change a password we enter the command

```
$ passwd
```

and get the responses

```
Changing password for NewUser
Old password:
```

After entering our current password, provided that this is entered correctly we receive the further prompt

```
New password:
```

and, after entering this, get yet another prompt (for a check):

```
Retype new password:
```

If this is consistent with the previous new value for the password, then it becomes permanently changed. If, however, we make a mistake in one of them then we get the line

```
Mismatch - password unchanged.
```

and our password remains unaltered. Of course, during all of this the password values are never echoed on the screen; however, the normal terminal functions such as 'delete' will still work.

3.8 Special characters

At this point it is relevant to mention one of the features of the UNIX *shell* that can cause considerable frustration, namely those characters which are styled the **metacharacters**. For the moment the purpose of mentioning them is simply so that the programmer can avoid getting entangled with them, and their actual uses will be described at a more appropriate point in Chapter 5.

The UNIX *shell* uses a number of printing characters as **command characters**, in addition to the control characters already mentioned. Since we may also wish to give these printing characters their normal meaning on occasion, there needs to be a method of disabling their special functions when necessary. The position is also a little clouded in that one or two of the interactive programs such as the text editor also use special characters, but not necessarily the same set as those used by the *shell*! Fortunately the method for disabling their effects is identical in all cases.

To concentrate for the moment upon the *shell*, the special characters (or **metacharacters**) are the set

```
; & ( ) | < > 'return' 'space' 'tab' * ? [ ]
```

The uses for 'return' (or 'newline') and 'space' have already been described in terms of formatting command lines, and the 'tab' character is an acceptable alternative to 'space' as a field delimiter.

We can turn off the effect of one of these metacharacters at any one point by using what is effectively another one, namely the '\' character. Placing this immediately before the metacharacter that we wish to disable will remove its special effects and leave it as an ordinary printing character. (We disable the effect of '\' in the same way within a string by using the form '\\'.) The use of '\' in this way is often referred to as **quoting** and the metacharacter so treated is referred to as having been **quoted**. For the *shell*, strings of characters enclosed within single quote marks are automatically quoted, as in

```
'a typical text string & comment line'
```

so that the '&' in this case would have no special effect. If the string is quoted using double quote marks, '""', instead, then the metacharacters within will retain their special effects.

It is important to know which characters are metacharacters, even though at this stage they will not be required. Just by knowing which characters they are we can avoid the occasional odd effect from time to time!

3.9*   Changing the *shell*

In an earlier section the *shell* was described as performing a number of 'housekeeping' tasks before giving the user a prompt to begin the terminal session. One of these tasks is to search the user's directory for a file with the name

```
.profile
```

and if this is found, then the *shell* executes the set of commands that it finds within that file. This uses a facility with which we will not be concerned until Chapter 7, namely programming the *shell* via command files, but the main point is that it allows some local tailoring of a user's environment to be automatically performed each time they log on. When more familiar with UNIX it is worth setting up your own '.profile' file. The actions that we can use this to perform can also be performed interactively at the terminal, and a particularly useful one is mentioned in the next few paragraphs.

3.9.1   Prompts

One very easy thing that we can do is to change the primary and secondary *shell* prompts from their default values of the '$' and '>' characters, to be any strings of characters that we choose. Although the *shell* is a special process, it is still a process which runs under the control of the system and which has been created from a program image. Some of the variables of this program, the **shell variables**, can be easily changed by the user. For the two prompts, the appropriate variables are

```
PS1 and PS2
```

and these can be changed by using a simple assignment statement. So if we prefer to have the string 'next_please' as our primary prompt instead of the '$', we type in the command

```
$ PS1=next_please
```

and will then be prompted by the string 'next_please' until we log off or reset PS1 to some other value.

While this example is very simple, it does show how even such minor things can be easily tailored to a form that you want. With practice, most users soon find a number of useful functions that can be performed for them by the '.profile' file.

3.10 Summary

This chapter has developed the main points in the important task of communicating with UNIX, and concerned itself with the fundamental tasks of terminal handling protocols and the means of issuing commands to the *shell* itself. In particular it has described the functions involved in

logging on to the system
correcting keyboard errors
running utility programs
logging out from the system
changing password and prompts

References

The more powerful aspects of the *shell* and examples of setting up a '.profile' file are well covered in the UNIX V7 document *An Introduction to the UNIX shell* by S R Bourne. They are also summarised in the entry for 'sh' in Volume 1 of the UNIX V7 Reference Manual. (Use the command

```
$ man 1 sh
```

to display this.)

The authoritative text on the subject is *The UNIX System*, Bourne S R, Addison-Wesley, 1982.

4
A bit about files

Keywords

cd; *chmod*; directory; file extensions; filename substitution; filestore; group; i-node; *mkdir*; protection bits; root; subdirectory; super-user

4.1 Introducing the filestore

An important feature in the design and use of any operating system is the ways in which it handles 'files', and the ease with which these can be created, changed and used by the user. Before seeing how this is done by UNIX, we should first briefly review just what is meant by the concept of a 'file'.

No computer of the present generation can handle (or the users afford) sufficient memory to hold simultaneously all of the programs and data that each user wishes to have available to him. So some form of bulk **backing store** or **filestore** has to be used to hold the programs and data, with the appropriate elements being copied into the computer's memory when needed. On the earliest systems the filestore was usually in the form of reels of magnetic tape, whereas today it is almost always some form of rotating magnetic disc, from the very large-capacity **Winchester disc** to the slow but cheap **floppy disc**. All of these provide the programmer with a means of storing programs and data as individual units, and to identify each of these units we have the idea of the **file**.

The file allows us to refer by a symbolic name to some area of a disc that the operating system has allocated to hold our information, of whatever type. Different operating systems use varying conventions for the naming of files, as well as different methods for allocating the physical blocks of the storage device to the file—hence the difficulty usually experienced in transferring data between apparently compatible computer systems. This forms a major difference between different operating systems, and includes various consequences as its corollaries. An important point about the file concept is that as a user we need to know nothing at all about the physical organisation of our data on the disc, or about the disc itself: type, volume, number of recording surfaces, etc. We only need to know the names of our files in order to be able to access the data that they contain, in a program-usable form. It is the task of the operating system to recognise any references that we or our programs make to a file by its name, and to convert those references into the appropriate disc block accesses and addresses.

The ways in which an operating system handles its filestore—a name which emphasises this detachment from the physical aspects of data storage—are very important to the user since nearly all of the functions that were identified in Chapter 2 involve accessing and using files in one way or another. For almost all applications we will need to be able to create files, modify them, compile their contents (so producing more files), and finally to run the processes which are formed from these and which will in turn handle data that is also likely to be stored in files.

The ease with which a user can access and maintain files is a very important feature of a system. It is also likely to be a much more important feature than the speed with which the files are accessed by the computer (unless this is exceptionally poor). Human responses are so much slower than those of the machine that we are usually much more inconvenienced by poor file handling facilities than we are by relatively slow speed of access to a file. (Actually, implementing file systems is quite a complex exercise, with a number of parameters which have to be balanced in some way when considering the organisation of the disc accessing. We will not concern ourselves with such points in this chapter.)

We have already seen one example of how a user's share of the filestore is manipulated, in the examples of Chapter 3, and Fig. 3.1 showed how the files making up the parts of the filestore used by the user 'NewUser' could be identified. Typical names were such as 'xray.f', i.e. no mention of any physical details about the filestore—just a name. So let's consider a bit more about how UNIX handles its filestore.

4.2   The UNIX filestore

On the UNIX system a **file** possesses certain **attributes** (chiefly a name, some information about such physical details as size, and some information showing who may access or change the file), and there is little more to it than the physical buffer on the device which is used to hold the actual contents of the file. The only internal structure that UNIX files possess will be any which has been created by the user and his programs. UNIX imposes no particular internal structures and simply regards each file as being a string of **bytes** (eight-bit items of information). If this is not a totally unique view of filestore, it is nonetheless an unusual one, as many operating systems have standard ways of internally structuring files, even though this may only be evident to the user in the form of some possible restrictions on line length, etc.

This does not mean that UNIX simply abandons the file to the user once space in the filestore has been allocated for it. Most utility programs such as the text editor, compilers, etc. will all use (and impose) some fairly simple formats for the files that they create—and of course they must do so in order to be able to exchange these files between one another. What it does mean is that if the text editor creates a file which contains lines of characters (or **text**), with each line terminated by pressing 'return', then this is exactly how the data will be stored in the file, including the storage of the 'return' character. The file handling processes will not reorganise it in any way behind the scenes.

This means that files are not subject to any artificial constraints when it comes to using them. The editor can read and modify any text files that use the standard internal structure adopted by the editor, regardless of which program created the file. (This is not always true for other file systems, where special **flags** may be secretly attached to a file. One suggested test for such hidden flags is to write a simple file copy program in FORTRAN (say), and to use this program, once compiled, to make a copy of its own source version into another file. Then see whether the compiler will accept this copy as its input. You may be surprised by the result of doing this on some systems; even where there appears to be no difference between the old and the new source files, the compiler will still not accept the new one!)

It may help to think of a UNIX file as being rather like a blank sheet of paper. We can write on it by ruling some lines and writing along them. This is what the UNIX utility programs do when they impose a simple internal format on their files [i.e. by using a line terminator (the 'return' character) to indicate the end of a 'line' of text]. The significant point though is that on many operating systems the lines are already there, and while the paper is generally convenient to use, any slightly different form of use becomes difficult to achieve.

When writing your own programs on UNIX, there is usually no lack of file handling support in the form of convenient input/output routines. There is no need to be concerned about having to 'rule lines'; these routines will perform the task for you. But when you eventually need to structure the file in some special way, then this flexibility is available (generally via some rather more primitive input/output routines). Until that occurs, just use the system as you would use any similar one, and without worrying about how the system does the file storage.

4.2.1 File naming conventions

There were some examples of filenames in the previous chapter, e.g. 'xray.f'. Each file that a user owns must have a name which is unique within the user's group of files, but beyond that requirement there is relatively little restriction on the form that names may take. A filename is simply an ordered string of printing characters, and can have any length between one and fourteen characters (you can use more, but the system only stores the first fourteen of them and ignores the rest). So if you want to call a file

> `parallelepiped`

or

> `test.f_version1`

then you are quite free to do so. (But avoid using the metacharacters in a filename, and remember that while '.' is not a metacharacter, it is used by some programs to delimit the fields of a filename; see below.)

This relative freedom to choose names can be useful. On many systems there is less flexibility about dividing a name into a number of **fields**, and where these exist they must be of certain lengths. UNIX has no very strong conventions about fields at all, and especially about appending default extensions to a filename. That said, the basic utilities do recognise some fairly simple naming conventions as defaults, although these are usually easy enough to override when necessary.

Filename extensions
One common convention is that the character '.' (the **period**) is used to separate the main body of a filename from an **extension** part of it. For example, in the name 'xray.f' we have the main body of the filename, 'xray', and the extension field, '.f'. Commonly encountered extensions include:

.c for source programs written in the C language;
.f for source programs written in FORTRAN;
.s for source programs written in assembler language;
.o for compiled programs which are not yet runnable;
.out for runnable (executable) files.

The act of compiling the file named 'xray.f' with the FORTRAN compiler will produce the files

> `xray.o`
> `a.out`

from the compilation and linking stages, which are usually invoked as one command. (Remember—to run the program, we just type in the name of the executable file 'a.out' and the *shell* will copy this file into memory and use it to create a UNIX process. For example,

```
$ a.out
```

is all that is needed.)

Note that the **object** (compiled) filename was created simply by taking the main body of the input filename and changing the extension field from '.f' to '.o'. This is a fairly common practice among programs such as compilers, which create new files from a source file.

Versions of a file

UNIX does not support the tagging of filenames with any form of version number. Most programs, such as the text editor, will read in one version of a file and, after making changes to it, will copy out the new one into a file which replaces the first one completely. Unless we specifically rename our output, there is no standard way of preserving both the new and the old versions of the file.

This is standard UNIX practice. If we designate, as the file which is to receive a program's output, a filename which is already in use for a file in our directory, then the new file created will replace the old one, and the old one will be deleted. It makes for tidier directories, since we do not have various versions of a program lying around, although it does have the disadvantage that if we accidentally delete a file then we have deleted our only version of it. This may require a different form of personal organisation than is required for those operating systems which preserve all versions of each file and leave it to the user to clean up their filestore occasionally (such systems need some personal organisation to avoid having the filestore entirely filled up with unwanted files). A later example in this text suggests a fairly simple way of maintaining a backup copy of source files, and facilities such as this may be useful as a means of protecting our more valuable files.

4.3 Directories

Almost any operating system will provide each user with his own **directory**. This generally takes the form of a special file which is associated with that user, and which contains assorted information about the files that he owns. Any form of reference that we make to a file owned by another user will also need to identify their directory as a part of the full identification of the file, so that the system can locate the correct one. On UNIX this idea of the directory is taken to its logical conclusion, and a directory is just another file on the system, with only its usage making it in any way different from an ordinary file.

[There *are* some other minor differences from other files. Like any operating system, UNIX has to maintain a lot of housekeeping information in order to support the file system, although this is usually hidden from users. A commonly encountered concept is that of the **file header** in which the system keeps information about the file; the user can obtain information from this file header, and can change some of the stored information via the utility programs, but has no other means of accessing it directly. There is usually a file header for each file on the file system. On UNIX the equivalent of the file header is provided by an item known as an **i-node**, a block of filestore (64 bytes) in which the system keeps information about a file. This information includes a **flag** area in which one of the flags is used to indicate whether or not this particular file is a directory. Apart from having this one flag set, the i-node for a directory will have the same form as it would for any other file.

As with other UNIX files, no structure is built into the directory, its internal structure being maintained by the appropriate utility programs and the file handling functions that we call from our own programs. We generally use *ls* to get a nicely formatted list of the files that we own from our directory, but some of the information could be obtained by using *cat* to print the raw contents of the directory. The format would be less attractive, and there are some non-character data parts that have funny effects on the printing device, but the basic point is that the directory can be accessed by any normal file handling process, not just by special ones. It is perhaps worth noting too that the directory does not contain any pointers to physical disc addresses. Instead, for each file entry it holds the filename as a string of characters and a simple number, the **i-number**, which serves to identify the appropriate i-node used for the file, and which in turn provides the information about the physical blocks being used on a disc.]

4.3.1 Subdirectories

One major advantage of the UNIX view of a directory as yet another file is that it easily leads on to the idea that if a directory is a file, then there is no reason why some of its own files cannot be directories too. It is precisely this facility for creating and using **subdirectories** that forms one of the most powerful and useful features of the file handling system.

We often find it easy to think of file systems as having 'tree-like' structures, and the analogy is quite a good one. We can see the user's directory as a minor branch of the whole file system, and its files being the 'twigs', as in Fig. 4.1. Figure 4.2 shows how for

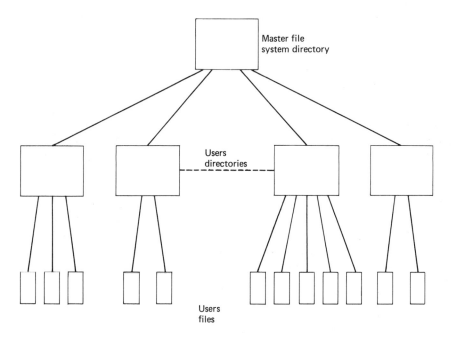

Fig. 4.1 A conventional file structure

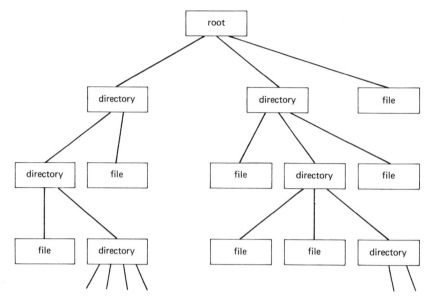

Fig. 4.2   The UNIX file structure (files and directories are indistinguishable except by their function)

UNIX this can be extended to the idea that the user's directory is simply a branch at any level of the tree, and that we can continue to have sub-branches to any depth beyond that, with twigs appearing alongside at any level. In practice it is rarely particularly advantageous to take the structure of our subdirectories down more than about three levels, since this provides for most groupings of our files and further depths can begin to make filename specifications unduly lengthy and hence error-prone.

An example of the usefulness of this scheme occurs when a user is working on more than one project. By creating a subdirectory for each project he is then able to group the files for each project together, and so keep apart from the files being used for different projects. This removes the need to use naming conventions to separate files within a directory. In addition, within these subdirectories, some of the specialist files such as documentation files can be further grouped within another level of subdirectory.

4.3.2   Creating directories

Files are constantly being created by many programs. Directories need to be explicitly created by the user and this task is performed by using the utility program *mkdir*. Supposing that we are again logged on as 'NewUser', let's see how this can be done.

Suppose that when we begin this working session, our directory contains the three files

```
newprog.f
test.dat
xray.f
```

after creating a subdirectory called 'project' via the command

```
$ mkdir project
```

a repeat of the command

```
$ ls
```

will give the list

```
newprog.f
project
test.dat
xray.f
```

with nothing to indicate that 'project' is a directory rather than an ordinary file. However, should we list our files with more information by using

```
$ ls -1
```

then this will change, and the entry for 'project' will be

```
drwxrwxr-x  2  NewUser          256  Jan 10  15:30  project
```

At the beginning of the line of information about the 'file', we now find the letter 'd' in place of the usual dash '−'. This 'd' is the indication that 'project' is really a directory and this flag will be recognised by any file handling programs and by any input/output routines called by our programs. (For example, the utility program *rm* will refuse to delete a directory.)

Having created our directory 'project', the next thing is to examine the means available for using it. If we want to begin by moving the file 'xray.f' from the main directory into 'project', then we can do this via the command

```
$ mv xray.f project/xray.f
```

and the string 'project/' will indicate that 'project' is the destination directory for the file, rather than the default directory which is our main directory. Figure 4.3 shows how our file structure will now appear if it is drawn out as a 'tree'.

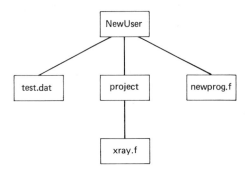

Fig. 4.3   The final directory and file structure for the example of Section 4.3.2

We can use this general form of

```
directoryname/<filename>
```

to refer to any file in the subdirectory, and should we choose to create at a later stage a further subdirectory of 'project', perhaps called 'documents', then we can refer to any file in that subdirectory by extending the form to

```
project/documents/<filename>
```

This form can be extended as far as is necessary to describe the tree of directories that we are using; directory names appear in descending order, with each name being a sub-directory of the one before it.

We can check the contents of our subdirectory 'project' by simply typing in

```
$ ls project
```

This will give the one entry

```
xray.f
```

Of course we can use an option such as '–l' for a fuller description of the contents if required.

When we want to work with the files in our subdirectory, having to use this rather lengthy file description soon becomes inconvenient. So UNIX provides another utility program, *cd*, which allows us to change the current 'working directory' which is to be searched as the default directory whenever we refer to a file. To make 'project' into the **default directory**, or **current directory**, for this purpose we enter the command

```
$ cd project
```

and now if we type

```
$ ls
```

then we will just get the entry

```
xray.f
```

as the contents of the current directory. Any files that we now create, using the text editor or any other program, will be entered into the directory 'project'. To return to our original directory (i.e. the one that we first acquired when logging on), we type the command

```
$ cd
```

and this use of *cd* with no arguments will always return us to the original directory, however many times we have changed our current directory in the meantime.

Another useful form is

```
$ cd ..
```

which returns us to the 'parent' of our current directory—i.e. one place up the tree.

Since sub-directories are directories of exactly the same form as our original default directory, we can expect that this too is a subdirectory of another directory on the system, and that our files are more fully to be described as

```
NewUser/<filename>
```

or, to give a specific example

```
NewUser/project/xray.f
```

This leads us into our next topic.

4.3.3   Directory trees

We can develop the arboreal analogy still further. In the same way that all of the branches of a tree radiate from one point, so all of the directories within the UNIX filestore lie on paths which branch out from a single directory. This directory is known as the **root** directory and is denoted by the single character '/' appearing at the beginning of a file specification.

Our own default directory that we use after logging on to the system is likely to be several layers removed (or branches 'up') from the root directory. Indeed, we do not expect that the root directory will contain many files other than directories amongst its entries. Given this, the full specification of one of our files is likely to be of the form

```
/.../..../.. ../NewUser/project/xray.f
```

The number of directories closer to root, and their names, are dependent upon a particular installation's choice of organisation for the filestore. Figure 4.4 shows a pictorial example of this.

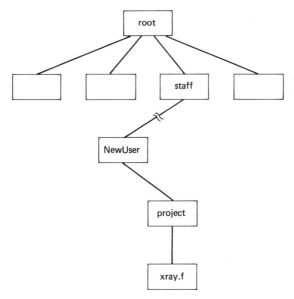

Fig. 4.4   The full directory tree for the file 'xray.f'

Some of the directories which appear in the root directory are standard features of the operating system. Two particular ones that we will meet again are

```
/bin
```

which is used to hold the files containing the executable run-time images for most of the system utility programs, and

```
/usr/bin
```

which holds a further group of these, and which by convention is also used to hold any that have been modified or produced locally. (Note that when searching for a file, the search path of the *shell* will normally cause it to search /bin before /usr/bin; so if any modified forms of programs are stored in the latter, the originals in /bin must be removed so that the modified forms will be found.)

We need not further concern ourselves with the subject of directories for the present. The flexibility of its filestore structure is one of the strengths of UNIX, and the use of subdirectories provides a useful resource for supporting various needs as will emerge more strongly when we come to look at building our own programs on UNIX.

4.4 File protection

On a multi-user operating system we may require to be able to control in some way the degree of access to our files that is permitted to other users of the system. We may have some files that need to be made available for others to read or copy, especially where we are working with other users on some shared project, and equally we may have files that we do not want other users to be able to access in any way.

UNIX gives us the means to tag our files with some information about who may have access to them, and what sort of access they are permitted to have. Control of the form of the access is important, since while we may want others to be able to read a particular file that we own, we do not necessarily want them to be able to write to it as well. The set of tags that can be applied to each file takes the form of nine **protection bits** or **attributes**, made up of three groups of three bits, and used to define three classes of user together with three forms of access for each class. These bits are checked by the low-level file handling processes whenever a user process requests access to a file in the filestore, in order to determine whether or not the user has the appropriate permission to access the file in the requested manner.

4.4.1 The three classes of user

The three classes of user, for each of which we may set a group of three protection bits, are:

> ourselves, as the owner of the file;
> any other users in the same 'group' as ourselves;
> all users of the system.

It may not be obvious why we might want to protect a file against ourselves. The reason is that this provides a means of preventing ourselves from accidentally deleting or overwriting a file that we wish to keep unchanged. When we finally do want to delete the file, we are of course able, as the owner of the file, to change the protections accordingly.

The user's group is something that is defined by the system manager locally when creating the entries for new users on the system. Besides allocating each user a unique **user identity number** (never seen or used directly by a user), each user is also given a **group identity number**. All users sharing the same value of the group identity number are considered to form a **group** on the system, purely for the purposes of the file access attributes. This idea of the group can be a rather useful feature where several people are working together on some project and need to be able to access one another's files, while denying access to any other users who are not involved in the work.

4.4.2   The protection bits

There are three of these attributes for each class of user, and they can usually be referred to by single letters when changing them or listing out their values for a file (use 'ls –l' for this). The three attributes that a file can possess for each class of user are:

r   for permission to 'read' a file;
w   for permission to write to a file (including the ability to delete it);
x   for permission to execute or run a file (only meaningful for an 'a.out' or *shell* program file).

Usually when these are listed, as by the command

```
$ ls -l
```

the presence of a letter indicates that the particular class of user possesses that attribute or permission; the absence of the letter, indicated by the use of the '–' character, indicates the lack of permission.

Any combination of these bits can be set for a file, and for each of the three classes of user. The example given in Fig. 3.1 shows the full listing of the information for each file in the directory. The access permission for the file's owner, group, and all users are given in that order. Normally a file is created with a set of **default attributes**, usually chosen so as to provide

rw   access for the owner and his group
r   access for all other users.

(If the file is an executable one, then the 'x' attribute is usually provided for the owner and their group too.)

We can change the protection of a file that we own by using the program *chmod*, which enables us to set or clear the protection bits for each class of user and type of access. The arguments of *chmod* are symbolic; the first one defines which classes of user are concerned with this change ('u' for user; 'g' for group; 'o' for other), while the second (normally signed), defines the attribute which is being changed—the sign indicating whether it is being removed or granted. For example

```
$ chmod go-wx <filename>
```

removes permission to write to or execute the given file for other members of the user's group and for other users of the system. While there is no need to use *chmod* while learning about the system, it is likely to prove a useful program once a user begins to create and use files in earnest.

4.4.3   Protection bits and directories

Since directories are files too, they also possess a full set of protection bits, though the interpretation given to the access modes is slightly different to that given to normal files (the classes of user are of course the same). For a directory, the 'rwx' bits are interpreted as:

r   for permission to read the directory as a file, i.e. to find which filenames are contained within it;
w   to create and delete files in that directory (needs **x** to be set too);

x   to search the directory for a given file (unlike the 'r' bit, this actually gives access to the files themselves).

One convenient feature of being able to create one's own subdirectories is that any files which need to be kept away from the sight of others, including possibly the rest of the members of the group, can be kept in a secure subdirectory to which only you as the user have access. However, as section 4.4.4 makes clear, for ultimate security you must also encrypt a file (see Chapter 5).

4.4.4   The super-user

Like almost any large multi-user operating system, UNIX possesses a particular user identifier which has special privileges and which can override the protection schemes of normal users when it is felt necessary to do so for the well-being of the system. This identity is known as the **super-user** and will normally be the owner of the root directory mentioned earlier, as well as of many of the system's more important files. You cannot protect your files against access by the super-user, (although encryption allows you to avoid having their contents read). This may of course be useful when you accidentally 'lock yourself out' by forgetting your password, since the super-user can reset it, (although not decode it). The reverse situation is certainly not true and the super-user can protect the system files as it wishes, the normal form being to grant users the 'r' and 'x' access attributes wherever possible but to keep the 'w' attribute for the few files where it is really necessary.

The super-user is a very necessary part of the system, but because of the power that it provides, it is important that the password used to give access to it is changed regularly and is only known to the few people who run the system.

4.5   A few utility programs

This section summarises the actions of some of the utility programs that are frequently used when manipulating files on UNIX. Most of them have already been mentioned, but it is helpful to have a reminder of their purposes at this point. In no very particular order they are as follows.

ls   lists directory contents and optionally provides various other details about each file held in the given directory.

cp   makes a copy of one file to another.

mv   renames a file and/or moves it to another directory. The original file identity is lost.

cat   lists the contents of a source file on the user's terminal. (It isn't very fussy and will try to list the contents of any file; though binary image files tend to produce funny effects on the screen!)

rm   deletes a file.

mkdir creates a new directory as a subdirectory of the current directory that is in use.

rmdir deletes a directory, but only if it is empty (i.e. contains no files or subdirectories).

cd   changes the current directory; if an argument is given then this directory becomes the current directory, and if no argument is given then the original directory with which the session began becomes the current directory.

chmod   changes the protection bits for a given file or directory.

There are obviously many others that could be included in this list, since almost all utility programs work with files in some way, but these represent a good basic group that allow one to make effective use of the UNIX filestore facilities.

4.6   Filename substitution (wildcards)

Strictly speaking, this is a facility which is provided by the *shell* rather than being a feature of the file system itself. However, this is an appropriate point at which to introduce it.

When the *shell* scans a filename that has been given to it, usually as an argument for a program such as those just described, it will check for the presence in the filename of any of the special characters

*   ?   [ ]

If one of these is detected, then the string of characters making up the filename will be treated as being a pattern for a filename, rather than the name of a specific file, and when the filename is passed to the program itself, it will have been replaced by a list of the available filenames that match the given pattern.

The three special characters have the following meanings when used in a filename string.

*   matches any string of characters, including the null string.
?   matches any single character.
[. . .]   matches any of the enclosed range of characters '. . .' in turn. (If two characters appearing in the pattern in alphabetical order are separated by a dash ('–') then any character in the alphabetic range between these two characters will be matched.) In many ways this is a more selective version of the '?' form.

The use of these **wildcard** characters is best shown by giving some examples.

4.6.1   Matching any string

We can use the character '*' in forms such as

```
$ ls xray*
```

to obtain a listing of all the files in the current directory that have names beginning with the string 'xray'. For example, if any of the following files were in our current directory, we would expect these to be listed by the above command:

```
xray
xray.f
xray.o
xrayspec
```

Similarly the command

```
$ ls xray.*
```

would list just the files

```
xray.f
xray.o
```

since we have specified a larger part of our pattern for the filename. Of course the '*' can appear anywhere in the string, not just at the end, although in practice this is one of the more common forms of use for it. Another common form is given in the example

```
$ cat *.f
```

which will list out the contents of all files with '.f' as their final characters.

It may already be obvious that the use of these general forms can be rather hazardous when using the *rm* utility to delete files, since a large number of files can be deleted with a single command such as

```
$ rm xray*
```

The possibility of deleting rather more than might be intended is only too evident.

4.6.2   Matching any character

The character '?' is more specific than the '*' and will allow only one character to be substituted in its place in the string. For example, the command

```
$ ls x?ay
```

would be matched by any of the files

```
xbay
xray
xxay
```

and so on, but not by such names as

```
x.day
xpray
```

Similarly the command

```
$ ls x?a?
```

could produce something of the form

```
xbay
xcat
xrat
xray
xxax
xxay
```

and so on.

4.6.3   Selective character matching

The pair of characters [ ] gives a more selective (and useful) form of the '?' and allows us to restrict the range of character matching permitted. An example of how this might be used would be the command

```
$ cat progl[a,b,c,d].f
```

or its rather shorter and more convenient form

```
$ cat progl[a-d].f
```

either of which will produce a listing of the contents of the files

```
progla.f  proglb.f  proglc.f  progld.f
```

concatenated together in that order.

  This form can be especially useful when the task of constructing a program involves having to recompile a series of files after making a change to one of them. The judicious choice of the filenames makes it possible to specify the compilation command with a single template in the command line, which may look something like

```
$ f77 -c xray[1-6].f
```

and which would compile the contents of the six files named xrayl.f through xray6.f in that order.

The examples given are all quite simple ones, and of course the forms may be combined to give very complex options. When using any of them with the *rm* utility, it is a wise precaution to use the '–i' option to ensure that you are requested to confirm each deletion before it is made. As an example of this, the command

```
$ rm -i *f
```

will generate the request

```
<filename>:
```

for each file with a name that matches the given string, i.e. a name which ends with the character 'f'. Pressing 'return' will cause the file to be preserved and not deleted. To delete the file enter 'y'.

  Many of the examples of later chapters use the last form given since, as indicated, it can be very useful when building programs or documents up from a number of files. It is well worth taking some trouble to choose filenames that make its use convenient in order to save time and typing errors as a program develops.

4.7 Devices

The UNIX system provides the software needed to control most of the more common peripheral devices available: discs; magnetic tape drives; line printers; terminals; etc. To allow flexibility of use, the program interfaces to these **device driver programs** take the same form as those to any normal file in the system, so making device access at the program level essentially indistinguishable from normal file access. This enables very flexible routing of program input and output, and the feature can be easily exploited to make many utility programs much more powerful than is initially apparent from a description of their functions.

More important still, it makes it possible for us to write all of our programs so that they are not concerned with the physical forms of their 'sources' and 'sinks' of data—a powerful form of logical abstraction. When using UNIX we should have no need to embed in our program any information about disc types or drive numbers. Simply assigning the appropriate 'file' and directory at run time will determine which physical device or part of filestore is to be used.

This aspect of flexible routing will be developed much further in Chapter 7, but for now this should suffice to explain the approach that UNIX takes to the question of device identification and use.

4.8 Summary

The relative importance of file handling on a system such as UNIX, and the many features that need to be described, have inevitably made this into a long and detailed chapter. It is important that this should not be allowed to obscure the basic point about UNIX file handling, which is the way in which its simple view of the file as a block of filestore to be used and structured allows us greater freedom to use files as we wish rather than as the system permits us. In the following chapters we will encounter software tools that exploit this freedom of choice. UNIX is a system designed for practical use, and this is particularly evident in its filestore handling.

While learning to use UNIX, much of the detail can be set aside until needed and a user can make very extensive use of the system without being concerned with the nature of the mechanism beneath.

5
Text editing

Keywords

append; change; current position; delete; *ed*; encrypt; global; insert; metacharacter; quit; quote; *sed*; substitute; text buffer; write

5.1 Introduction

It has been said of the game of Mah Jong that there are about as many versions of the rules as there are players of the game. The subject of text editing programs (commonly called simply **editors**) seems to be in the same league. Everyone has their own ideas about what features they consider should be provided in the ideal interactive text editor program—and these ideas always seem to be a little different from those preferred by anyone else. (Here **text** is simply taken to refer to strings of characters, whether these make up the source code of a program or a document of some kind.)

On UNIX the issue of the variety of editors is further compounded by the relative ease with which new software tools may be constructed and existing ones modified. When combined with the added facilities that many VDUs can now also provide, it is not unusual for installations to be using a 'standard' editor all of their very own. Before getting too deeply into this chapter it may be prudent to check what flavour (or flavours) of text editor is supported on your local UNIX system.

UNIX V7 provides two fairly basic but powerful text editor programs. The main one is *ed*, which is the interactive text editor, while the second, *sed*, is intended for use as a **stream editor**, taking its commands from a **steering file** and used for editing very large files or for very repetitive work. In the UK at least, users are likely to have access to *em*, which is a more user-friendly variant on the general theme of *ed*. (In this context, 'user-friendly' principally means that *em* actually issues prompts to the user!) *ed* does not issue any prompts to the user when expecting commands from the keyboard, a feature that can be disconcerting at first and makes *ed* an editor which is never really likely to be particularly well loved!

The rest of this chapter concentrates upon how we can make simple use of the standard interactive editor *ed* to create and modify files of text, since *sed* is not a software tool that the new user will immediately need. Anyone with access to *em* will find this chapter relevant too, but will have the benefit of some prompts to help them along. The examples that are given are very simple, and will show how a file can be created and modified using only a simple set of commands and command formats.

5.2 Creating a text file

The sequence of actions that are needed to create a new file of text is quite simple. Having invoked the editor we enter our 'text' into its buffer and then when this is complete we direct it to copy the contents of the memory buffer out to a given file.

The editor is invoked in the usual way, by entering the command

```
$ ed
```

and we can then proceed to give it commands. (The lack of a prompt from *ed* to indicate that it is awaiting commands can be rather unnerving at first, since after typing in the command to run the editor there will be no further responses from the system to indicate that anything is happening at all!)

To enter some text we need only one command, the **append** command, consisting of the letter 'a' followed by pressing the 'return' key. (All of the *ed* commands have this terse one-character form.) From then on, every line that we type in will be stored, in order, in the editor's buffer until we signify the end of the append by entering a line which contains a single period '.' as the first and only character, followed by a 'return'. This will have the effect of returning *ed* to command mode again, although of course there will be no indication of this.

For example, the sequence of commands needed to run the editor and to enter the lines

> The aim of First Aid is to obtain medical aid
> immediately and to combat shock.

into the editor's memory buffer is shown below.

```
$ ed
a
The aim of First Aid is to obtain medical aid
immediately and to combat shock
.
```

More lines can be further appended after these two by entering an 'a' again and continuing as before. A block of text can be as long as desired although until a greater familiarity with using *ed* is acquired, most users may prefer to work with fairly short blocks of lines, checking the entries made as they go.

Having entered the lines of text into the editor's buffer, the remaining actions are to copy the contents of the buffer into a file and then to terminate the editing session and return to the *shell*. For these actions we need two more *ed* commands, namely

w   the **write** command

q   the **quit editor** command.

When giving the 'w' command we must also specify a filename for the new file which will be created to hold the copy of the buffer. This is given as a parameter of 'w'; for example

```
w gamma.f
```

which will copy the contents of the buffer into a file called 'gamma.f' (presumably in this case the buffer contains the source for a FORTRAN program). For once, *ed* gives a response to a command, by printing the count of characters that were transferred; and if we forget to specify the filename, and have not specified one previously in the editing session, then we will get a response of '?'.

Issuing a 'w' command does not affect the contents of the buffer in any way; they are simply copied, and so we can continue to make further changes and additions to them, possibly including more 'w' commands as we go. Faced with a lengthy editing session this may be a good practice to adopt; even given the very stable nature of UNIX V7 it is wise to take some precautions against an error of any form. Note too that after the first use of 'w', if we do not specify a filename as an argument to following 'w' commands, they will continue to use the filename first given, overwriting previous versions of the file on each occasion.

The quit editor command, 'q', instructs the editor to terminate the present editing session and to return control to the *shell*. If the contents of the memory buffer have been changed in any way since the previous 'w' command was issued, then *ed* will check that you really do want to quit and lose these changes. It does so by typing the usual '?' and waiting for a response. If you do intend to quit, then typing another 'q' will enforce this. Otherwise, simply type 'w' and then 'q' to copy the last changes out to the file before quitting.

Before ending an editing session you may like to check the contents of the editor's version of the file by listing it on the terminal screen. To do this simply enter the command

        1,$p

and the current contents of the buffer file will be listed on the screen. Here we see the use of the special character '$' to indicate the last line of the file.

A full editing session to create a new file (in this case a simple FORTRAN program) will look something like the following (the commands have been underlined to distinguish them):

```
$ ed
a
C         A SIMPLE FORTRAN PROGRAM
C
          WRITE(6,100)
          STOP
C
  100     FORMAT(X,'HELLO')
          END
.
w test.f
80
q

$
```

(Here '80' indicates that 80 characters were transferred to the file 'test.f'.) Now give it a try yourself.

5.3 Modifying a text file

Being able to make alterations to text files is every bit as important as being able to create them. This is especially true when using *ed*, as the lack of prompts is apt to result in files containing such lines as

```
w gamma.f
q
```

caused by forgetting to terminate the append, and then being unable to distinguish between append mode and command mode in the absence of a prompt!

Of course you can also make alterations, corrections and changes while first creating a file, but for the purposes of this section we will only consider the case where we are changing an existing file, since most files are only created once, but are modified many times.

To **open** an existing file in order to make changes we begin as before by invoking the editor, but this time also giving, as a parameter, the name of the file that we wish to use. For example,

```
$ ed gamma.f
```

In this case, when the editor process is started up by the *shell*, its first action will be to copy the contents of the file 'gamma.f' into its memory buffer and to print out on the screen the number of characters that it has read from the file. For example, if we were now to read in the file that was created in the last section, 'test.f', the initial lines will look like this:

```
$ ed test.f
80
```

We can now go ahead and make whatever changes and additions we like to the contents of the editor's buffer before writing it back out to create a new version of 'test.f' or even a new file. If we simply use 'w' without specifying a destination filename, then the original name supplied as the parameter of the initial call will be used. The remainder of this section summarises a few of the facilities that can be used to make such changes.

5.3.1   Current position ('dot')

To help the user in accessing the editor's buffer, the editor maintains an internal scheme of line numbering. These numbers are purely for use within the editor and are not included in any way in the files that it creates. Each line in the buffer is given a number, beginning from 1 (*not* 0), and the editor keeps a constant note of our **current position** while accessing the buffer.

The idea of current position can be likened to a one line **window**; at any time this window is placed over one line of the buffer—the **current line**—and the current position is the line number of this line. While using the editor we can think of ourselves as moving the window around as we work on different lines, and the current position as always pointing to this window.

Some of the commands that we will be using can optionally be preceded with the number of the line that they are intended to affect. If not, then the default is that the command is to apply to the current line. The editor allows us to make symbolic reference to the current position at any time, via the character '.', which is sometimes referred to as 'dot'. At the start of the editing session, after the file has been copied into the editor's buffer, 'dot' will initially take the value of the last line to be read in. So if our file consists of twenty lines of text, the initial value of 'dot' will be 20. For much of the time, we are not concerned with the actual value of 'dot' since we will move it around by pattern matching and similar methods.

The current position is changed by any command that references another line in the buffer, however this is done. For example, we can print the contents of any line on the screen by just typing its line number. So to print the fourth line we just enter

4

The current position will be reset to 4 by this command, and any subsequent commands that do not specify a particular line will be applied to that line.

At any time we can display the contents of the current line by the command

.p

and can obtain the current value of 'dot' (i.e. the position of the line within the buffer) by the command

.=

In practice, while we occasionally use '.p', there is rarely much need for '.='.

We can advance the position of 'dot' by one line, and cause the contents of the new current line to be printed, simply by pressing the 'return' key with no command character at all. Similarly we can move the position of 'dot' back by one line by entering the command character '−', followed by 'return'. The two forms are a useful means of stepping through the buffer one line at a time.

At this point, we should also note that while many commands can only be issued on their own, and commands are separated by the use of 'return', the **print** command 'p', which we have just met, is an exception to this rule and can be appended after any command to ensure that the results of an action are printed out on the screen. In a command such as

4p

it would of course be superfluous, since just entering the line number will effectively incorporate the 'p'. In such cases, an added 'p' command will be ignored; i.e. the editor will not print out the line twice.

5.3.2   Finding a given string of characters

Even when working with an up-to-date listing of a file, and one which includes line numbers, it is not usually very convenient to move to every line of text that we are working upon by having to enter its line number. For example, while it is always good practice to work with a listing that is annotated with the changes that we wish to make, sometimes we also need to check that our visual scanning of the listing was complete. For such occasions the editor provides a 'search' command that allows us to specify the particular pattern of characters that we wish to locate in the buffer. Given such a pattern, it will then scan through the whole of the buffer until either a match for the pattern is found within a line or the whole buffer has been searched.

This feature is still useful even when we are using a line-numbered listing, since the line-numbering is positional, rather than tied to a line, and any additions to or deletions from the lines in the buffer will then change the line numbers of succeeding lines. Using the **search** facility is then a more practical form of working than trying to work out what the new line number of our line should be.

The search command is given by placing the string of characters that we wish to have used as the pattern between two '/' characters, as in

/null=0/

This particular command would then set the editor searching its buffer for the string 'null=0' appearing anywhere in any line. The search is made from the current position, and when the end of the buffer is reached the search wraps around and continues searching from the beginning until the original start point is reached. If no match is found for the pattern then the current position will remain unchanged and the editor will respond with the '?' character. If a match is found, then the current position will be reset to this new line and the whole of the new current line will be printed on the screen. In the above example we might find a line such as

```
if null=0 then
```

as our first match.

To minimise the number of false matches that the editor will find we should try to choose the pattern with some care, to avoid ambiguity. In the above example, had the file contained the line

```
if x>10 and charnull=0 then
```

preceding the actual string we were seeking, then this would have been found first and a better search pattern would have been

```
/if null=0/
```

instead.

As shown in this example, the first match that is found may not always be the one that we actually want. To search again using the same pattern we can simply type in the abbreviation

```
//
```

and the editor will continue the search. Take a little care if using this several times, since the editor can simply continue to find the same matches cyclically because of the wrap-around effect.

5.3.3   Adding more text (i and a)

A common requirement in editing is to add some more lines to a file, probably at various points between the existing lines. With many text editors there is a little confusion on first acquaintance as to whether the 'insert' command will place the new lines before or after the current line. Not so with *ed*, since this provides commands for both cases.

To **insert** lines of text BEFORE the current line we enter the command 'i', followed by 'return', and then enter our new lines, terminating with a line containing only the character '.' as in our previous example of 'a'. Similarly we **append** lines of text AFTER the current line by using the 'a' command that we have already met. Remember too that both of these will have the effect of renumbering any subsequent lines in the file.

5.3.4   Deleting lines (d)

We all make mistakes in our programs or keypunching (why else should we need such splendid text editors), and sometimes we need to remove a line or even a block of consecutive lines. The 'd' command is used for this and may be used in one of a number of formats.

We can delete the current line by typing in the one letter command

    d

However, since we would usually like some confirmation of the effects of this we can conveniently use the 'p' command's property of being used with others to make this into

    d p

This will print out the new current line, which should be the one that previously followed the line just deleted.

    To delete a line without first moving the current position as a separate action, we just type in the line number followed by the letter 'd', as in

    7 3d

which will delete the 73rd line of the buffer. Again, what was formerly the 74th line will now become the 73rd line, and hence the current line. Note that deleting lines in this way requires confidence that the line number has not been altered by previous editing.

    Another useful form, where we wish to delete a block of lines rather than just one line, is of the form

    <firstline,lastline>d

where we specify the first line and the last line of the block to be deleted and separate them by a comma, following with the 'd'. (This is a general form which can be used with many of the commands, but which is particularly useful with 'd'.) For example, the command

    5,9d

will have the effect of deleting from the buffer lines 5 to 9 inclusive. Since the effect is rather drastic, it may pay to check first that we have the correct lines, by listing them using the same form with 'p':

    5,9p

This will print on the screen lines 5 to 9 inclusive.

5.3.5   Altering lines of text (c and s)

ed supports two forms of alteration to a line. The first is concerned with replacing the whole line, while the second is concerned with replacing a part (or parts) of it.

    Where we need to replace a line completely with one or more new lines, the **change** command 'c' can be used. This has the same effect as using the 'd' command followed by the 'i' command; i.e. deleting the current line (or specified group of lines) and inserting the new ones. As with the 'i' and 'a' commands, we terminate the block of replacement lines with a line containing only a '.'. The 'c' command can be used to replace a block of lines rather as described for the 'd' command, by specifying the first and last lines of the block to be replaced. For example, the sequence

    6,12c
    this is the first new line
    and this the second
    .

will replace lines 6 to 12 in our file with the two lines containing

```
this is the first new line
and this the second
```

The lines following these will then be renumbered since we have replaced a block of seven lines by two lines.

While we can bypass the 'c' and use the 'd' and 'i' combination, there is no way of progressing very far without the **substitute** command. This is one of the most useful commands in *ed* and allows us to replace a part of a line of text with new text.

As with the search command, we need to be able to specify a pattern of characters that are to be replaced with a new pattern, and we use the same delimiter, the '/' character, to separate each of these. (If the '/' is a part of the string then it must of course be quoted.) For example, suppose that the current line is

```
the first and last items in the block
```

and we wish to change 'items' to read 'lines'. We would use the command

```
s/item/line/
```

to perform the substitution. The first string specified is that which is to be replaced, and the second is that which is to replace it. The second string can be a null string, specified by '//'. The 's' command is another case where the ubiquitous 'p' can usefully be appended so that we are able to check the effect of our alteration. This is a particularly sound practice to adopt since the substituted string will replace the first occurrence of the pattern that it finds along the line. (Remember that *ed* is a line-oriented editor, dealing with whole lines at a time, and does not allow us to step along a line in any way.)

An example of the point made above is given in the following example, where we have the mis-typed line

```
the ice axe plays an important rolle in the practice
```

and wish to correct the mis-spelt 'rolle' to 'role'. It would be tempting simply to use the command

```
s/l//p
```

but this would result in the line

```
the ice axe pays an important rolle in the practice
```

since it would match and remove the first 'l' encountered. In this case the correct command to use would be

```
s/ll/l/p
```

which would correctly reduce the double 'l' to a single letter.

If we make an error in typing in the pattern to be replaced, then the editor will return its usual '?' if it fails to find a match along the current line. The current line itself will not be altered on an error.

While the substitute will normally change only the first pattern match that it encounters along the line, we can also direct it to replace all matches along the line by appending a 'g' after the last '/' character. So the command

```
s/real/integer/gp
```

will change every occurrence of the string 'real' on the current line to be integer, and will then print out the new version of the line.

While the above set of editor commands are not by any means a complete summary of those actually available, they should be sufficient to get a new user started and effective, and as need arises the repertoire of *ed* commands can then be extended to meet it.

5.4 The metacharacters

In Chapter 3 we encountered the concept of metacharacters during the introduction to the UNIX *shell*; the metacharacter being a printing character which is treated in a special way, unless specifically disabled. Using the editor is the other common occasion with UNIX where we need to use certain characters with a degree of caution.

The editor actually uses two groups of special characters, and although only one of these groups can really be considered as metacharacters, we will discuss both groups in this section. The metacharacters are used to specify position along a line (the current line) and to aid certain pattern matching requirements. While we may not necessarily wish to use them while first learning how to use *ed*, we should know which characters they are so that we can avoid some rather unexpected effects.

5.4.1 Position of a line in the buffer

To deal with the special characters first, we have already encountered the two symbols '.' and '$' used to specify the position of a line, and we have considered various uses of '.'. (As a reminder, '.' signifies the line number of the current line, and '$' signifies the line number of the last line in the buffer.) Most of the forms described apply to '$' too. Like the '.' symbol, it can be used wherever we can use a line number in a command format. For example

```
$p
```

will print out the last line (and reposition the current line '.' to that line). To find the current value of '$' at any time, i.e. the number of lines in the buffer, we type

```
$=
```

or, more briefly,

```
=
```

This is similar to using '.=' to obtain the value of '.', as we did earlier.

A useful way of accessing lines within the buffer that is often used, especially with '$' and '.', is the **relative offset**. Besides referring to a line by its absolute position in the buffer (i.e. its line number), we can also refer to it by expressing its line number in terms of another line number plus or minus an offset, as in

```
some position+offset
```

or

```
some position-offset
```

where 'some position' is commonly '.' or '$'. As an example of use of this, the command

   $-5,$-1p

will print out the five lines of the buffer immediately preceding the last line, and leave '.' addressing the last line but one in the buffer. Similarly, at any time the form

   .-5,.+5p

will print out the eleven lines centred on the current position. The only catch to this is that this form will actually change the current position to the last line referred to, and so if necessary it must be moved back to the original line via the command

   .-5

This is so common a form that it can be further abbreviated to

   -5

Here we are using the form of the print command by which we specify the line number of the line to be printed, but using a relative form to do this rather than an absolute one. Using relative offsets is quite a useful way of moving around a particular part of the buffer, especially when making small changes to, say, a subprogram source text.

5.4.2   Position of text within a line

The use of metacharacters by the editor for the purpose of matching strings along a line in the search and substitute commands is very similar to that made by the *shell* in making wildcard substitutions for filenames. As it is unnecessary for initial basic use of the editor, the details of use will not be covered here.

It is necessary though to know exactly which characters are used for this purpose, and which must therefore be 'quoted' via the '\' character when being used as a part of a text string in the search or substitute commands. (These two commands, which are the commands which involve pattern matching, are the only times when we are concerned with metacharacters in the editor.) The characters concerned are:

   / . * $ & ? [ ] \ ^

As an example, since the character '/' is usually used as a delimiter of the patterns, it must be quoted itself if it is a part of the pattern. So we can end up with such commands as

   s/3\/4/5\/8/p

which will substitute the string '5/8' in place of the string '3/4'. (A useful point to remember about quoting is that if we accidentally type in the '\' character at any point, we then need to press the 'delete' key *twice* to remove it. This is because the first 'delete' will actually be 'quoted', and hence encoded into the editor's buffer, and the second 'delete' will then remove this!)

5.5*   Some other facilities of *ed*

This last section is intended to provide a brief review of some other features of the text editor *ed* which should be noted by the user, either for their potential usefulness or as possible pitfalls to be avoided.

5.5.1   Making multiple instances of a change

When making alterations to a program or document, it is sometimes useful to be able to repeat a particular substitution throughout the complete memory buffer, or at least within a given range of lines. The item changed may be a variable name, or a technical term, but the main point is that we want to change every occurrence of it and to avoid having to repeat this by hand if possible.

The **global** command, specified by the letter 'g' (and not to be confused with the 'g' used with the substitute command when changing all occurrences along a line) can be used to specify that the sequence of editor commands that follow it should be applied throughout the buffer. It takes the form

```
g/<string to be matched>/ <command list>
```

or if we want to restrict its action to a range of lines, the form

```
<firstline,lastline>g/<string to be matched>/ <command list>
```

In effect this command's arguments consist of the sequence

```
search ; action
```

where the 'g' indicates that the search and action parts are to be repeated until the range of lines specified has been exhausted. The search is in the form that we have already met and the action consists of one or more editor commands.

The command list that makes up the action part is often just one command, and most commonly it is the substitute command, as in the command

```
g/bell/s/bell/Bell/gp
```

which will seek out every occurrence of the string 'bell' in the buffer and change it to the string 'Bell', printing out the changed line in each case.

More powerfully, since the 'match' string is remembered, we can abbreviate this command to the form

```
g/bell/s//Bell/gp
```

and the '//' will then contain the original match string of 'bell'. This form of 'memory' also applies when we search for a string and then substitute, as in

```
/bell/
s//Bell/
```

Here, once the string 'bell' is found, it will then be used again as the match for the substitute and so the first occurrence of 'bell' will be replaced by 'Bell'.

We can extend the 'command list' to include more commands than the single one of the above example by entering the sequence of commands with each command on a separate line, terminating each line except the last with a '\' before the 'return'. The last line is terminated by 'return' alone, and this indicates the completion of the 'g' specification.

5.5.2   Sending commands to the *shell*

We can break out of the editor's command mode at any time, in order to send a one-line command to the *shell*, by prefixing the shell command with a '!' character. As an example, in entering a program which calls an independently compiled subprogram, which is in turn stored in another file, we may wish to make a check on the order or type of parameters that need to be used in calling the subprogram. We can conveniently do this by listing the source of our subprogram on the screen using *cat*, and then continue with our editing session. This can be done using the command

```
!cat subs.f
```

in order to list out the file 'subs.f'.

5.5.3   The 'W' command—a warning

The 'W' command is something of a booby trap, for the FORTRAN programmer in particular and sometimes for the assembler programmer too. Unlike the 'w' command, which copies the buffer out to a file and creates a new version of the file in doing so, the 'W' command will likewise copy the buffer to the given file—but will append it to the end of the existing contents of the file instead of creating a new version.

It represents a particular hazard for the FORTRAN programmer because of the long tradition of writing FORTRAN source programs in upper-case letters (although the UNIX version of the compiler, *f*77, will actually accept non-standard lower-case letters). When entering a program in this form, it is only too easy to leave the 'CAPS' key down when completing an edit—and thus type in a 'W' instead of a 'w'! Fortunately, since the problem is one of excess of output rather than a loss, it is not too difficult to remedy it with the editor—but it can lead to some rather baffling error messages if the mistake is not noticed before the file is passed to the compiler.

5.5.4   Encrypting the text file

The idea of encrypting strings of characters was encountered earlier when the storage of passwords was described. UNIX does provide a *crypt* utility program that allows the user to encrypt any source file (and decrypt it too of course) as a means of security. However, there is always the hazard in using this that forgetting the encryption key results in a rather useless file which no-one else (including the super-user) can retrieve.

The editor *ed* also has access to the facilities of *crypt* and can read and write encrypted files too. This facility is accessed via the 'x' command, which then asks for a key to be used in decrypting input files or in encrypting output files. Should you accidentally type 'x', then the editor will ask for a **key**. The response of entering just 'return' in reply will provide a null key, i.e. no encryption. Should your fingers be ahead of you and a key be accidentally entered in response to the prompt, then just type the 'x' again and enter simply a 'return' to reset the key to a null before performing any 'w' commands: encryption is not activated until the buffer contents are copied out to a file.

5.6   Summary

This chapter has described some of the facilities provided by the standard UNIX text editor, *ed*. There are different ways of using almost any text editor in order to perform the same tasks, and each user will no doubt find a set of commands that best suits their own methods of work. This chapter suggests some of the possible ways of performing various tasks, and with growing experience you can no doubt extend your vocabulary of editing skills to perform some of them in much more direct ways.

Table 5.1 shows a summary of the *ed* commands described in this chapter, together with others whose use should be self-evident.

Table 5.1 A summary of useful *ed* commands. There are many other commands which will prove useful in due course; consult the editor documentation for details of these.

Command	Action	Comment
a	Append text lines.	
i	Insert text lines.	
{x, y}p	Print lines x to y inclusive.	Default current line.
{x, y}l	Print lines unambiguously.	Includes non-printing characters.
{x, y}d	Delete lines x to y inclusive.	Default current line.
{x, y}c	Change lines x to y inclusive.	Equivalent to {x, y}d and i.
/ ... /	Search for pattern.	'No match' indicated by '?'.
s/xxx/yyy/{g}	Substitute pattern.	
{x, y}g	Repeat commands.	
w {filename}	Copy buffer to file.	
W {filename}	Append buffer to file.	
r {filename}	Read file to buffer.	Useful for merging files.
{x, y}mz	Reposition lines x to y inclusive after z.	

Reference

1. Kernighan, B W, *A Tutorial Introduction to the ED Text Editor*, UNIX V7.

6
Building programs

Keywords

Assembler; *as*; *ar*; C; *cc*; FORTRAN; *f77*; include files; *ld*; library files; link-editor; *lint*; *nm*; object files; *pcc*; *size*

6.1   A trio of languages

Whatever the reasons we may have for using a UNIX system, sooner or later we will probably want to write some programs of our own. Although a wide variety of programming languages have been implemented on UNIX systems, for this chapter we will concentrate only on the details of how to use those which are normally included as standard with UNIX V7.

C

A key feature of UNIX as an operating system is that so much of it is itself written in a high-level language—the language C. (Hence the relative ease with which UNIX has been made available on machines other than the PDP-11.) Despite being a language with the sort of features that are needed for writing system programs, and that are concerned with the control and use of machine features, C also provides the data typing and the structuring forms expected of a modern high-level language. Unfortunately it also possesses a rather excessive potential for extreme brevity of style too. But whether you prefer to view C as a form of portable assembler for system programming or as a high-level language that is oriented towards applications work, it is a very useful and versatile language—and as it was designed for the purpose of constructing UNIX, it is particularly well supported and documented on UNIX. Some personal discipline may be needed to avoid letting this potential for brevity lead to programs which are completely obscure!

FORTRAN

Within the scientific community, FORTRAN still retains a very strong hold, despite its lack of real structure and of data security; if only because of the sheer volume of investment that is represented by the many packages and libraries available for use with the FORTRAN language. The FORTRAN 77 standard is fully supported on UNIX— and the inevitable (and irresistible) extensions that all compiler writers feel obliged to add to FORTRAN have been kept within reasonable and useful bounds. Its use has been described fairly thoroughly in this chapter, since it is likely to be a familiar language for many readers.

Assembler

On any system there are always those few specialist requirements that need the use of an assembler, although the number that actually use it may seem rather more than the number that really need it. While UNIX does support an assembler (for the PDP-11 family), it is a rather grudging form of provision and only the very determined (or utterly unreformed) are likely to enthuse about its use. Given the facilities and power of C, this does not seem an unduly inadequate approach. The assembler is only given a very brief description in this chapter, as seems appropriate to its status under UNIX.

Other languages are likely to be available on an installation, and Pascal may even be available in several implementations. Since the sound engineering of programs requires the use of languages that are well structured and support modern concepts of information hiding, it is worth observing that the excellent practical derivative of Pascal, Modula-2, is also available under UNIX and capable of providing for a wide range of application programming. For the wholly unreformed and unrepentant there may even be some form of BASIC too!

Since the C language is very much a UNIX-based language, it is worth observing at this point that it is well described by a very good definitive text, which also covers its use within the UNIX environment. Only an outline description of the language is given here, and those who would like to, or need to, write C programs are referred to *The C Programming Language* by Kernighan and Ritchie. This chapter also assumes that the reader has some familiarity with DEC's own MACRO-11 assembler when describing the UNIX assembler *as*. (If you really want to learn to write in Assembler, then using *as*, or UNIX for that matter, is not really the best starting place!)

6.1.1   The C language

The C language was developed as a derivative of the system programming language BCPL (there was a 'B' language *en route* of course!). It provides an assortment of features, many of which will be fairly familiar to anyone who has ever programmed in an Algol-type language such as Pascal. Some important features include the following:

limited block structuring (giving some degree of scope control);
structured flow control constructs for branching, looping and multiple-way branches (if-then-else, for, while, switch etc.);
data typing (and creation of enumerated types);
use of pointers (in profusion!);
structures (rather akin to Pascal's *record* facility);
function procedures (in fact, all subprograms in C must be functions);
parameter passing to subprograms by **value** (for call by **reference** one must pass a pointer parameter by value);
library routines for input and output;
recursive subprograms.

The emphasis on support for system programming has led C to provide fewer checks and restrictions on the use of some of these features than might be expected from a more tightly structured language, and the C compiler is fairly permissive, especially where the use of pointers is concerned. A more rigorous check of a C source program can be obtained by running it through another UNIX utility program called *lint*. This checks the syntax of the program very thoroughly, and will even give warning of any potential pitfalls that it might contain. While *lint* generates no executable code, it does ensure that the programmer is aware of anything that might become a source of error.

[Besides the standard C compiler (the program name is *cc*), there is also a portable C compiler (named *pcc*, in a sudden outburst of logic on naming conventions).

Being a language designed for system writing, C has some features that are, if not machine-dependent, at least machine-influenced; but despite these, there is sufficient machine independence to allow compilers to be produced which will generate code to run on other makes of computer apart from the PDP-11. The portable C compiler differs from the standard C compiler in that it has been internally designed in such a way that the machine-dependent parts, including code generation, can be replaced by new versions without the need for major rewriting of the other parts. It is the existence of this version of the C compiler that has enabled the UNIX operating system to be implemented on machines other than the PDP-11 in a far less painful fashion than would be the case for almost any other operating system of its generation. It has also formed the basis for the production of various forms of cross-compiler for use in host–target developments.]

Figure 6.1 gives a short and simple example of a C program, to give some idea of the style and syntax of the C language for those who have not previously encountered it. It should be observed that the C syntax would have permitted this example to be written using fewer source statements, but at a significant cost in terms of its clarity to the reader.

6.1.2   FORTRAN 77

Despite the apparent emphasis on the C language within the UNIX culture, it is worth observing that many UNIX users have never written any programs in C and will probably never do so either. FORTRAN under UNIX is certainly a very real software tool, not just an afterthought, and indeed, UNIX is claimed to have provided the first full version of the ANSI FORTRAN 77 standard with its *f77* compiler.

As with almost any FORTRAN compiler, there are some local extensions to the ANSI standard in *f77*. These include the non-standard type DOUBLE COMPLEX and also the provision of recursion for subroutines and functions as a default. This latter feature comes as a bonus from the way that the compiler has been constructed to generate intermediate code for the C compiler, which of course does provide for recursive subprograms. Two extensions which can usefully be described in a little more detail at this point are the **include** feature and the **undefined** option.

'include' files
The 'include' feature might already be familiar to some readers as it now appears in various language implementations, including the C language, and in a number of operating systems. At any point within the source text of a program, the inclusion of a statement of the form:

```
include <filename>
```

will cause the compiler to begin reading its source statements from the new file specified by 'filename' until this has been exhausted, i.e. until it reaches the end-of-file marker. At that point the compiler returns to reading its input from the original file. This facility can

```
/*   program to read from the standard input and write to the
     standard output, passing text on a line by line basis
     until it encounters a line containing only a ".".

     for use with the comment proforma generator.
*/

     int ch,nch,flag;          /* data declarations for type integer */
     int linebuf[80];          /* declare an integer array */

/* the main body of the program follows - note that the pair { and }
are used to denote the BEGIN and END of a block or compound statement */

main()
{
     flag = 0;

     while (flag==0)
     {
         readline();
         if (flag==0) writeline();
     }
}

/* now the two procedures to read and write a line of characters   */

readline()       /*read one line of text */
{
     nch = 0;
     while ((ch=getchar()) != '\n' )   /* \n is the 'return' character */
         linebuf[nch++] = ch;
     if (( nch==1 ) && (ch = '.'))
         flag = 1;
     else
         linebuf[nch] = '\n';
}

writeline()      /* write one line of text */
{
     int count;
     putchar('\t');          /* add tab at start of line */
     for (count=0 ; count <= nch ; count++ )
         putchar(linebuf[count]);
}
```

Fig. 6.1   An example C program

be extremely useful when constructing a large program from a number of independently compiled source modules, all or some of which need to be compiled using a set of standard declarations of constants and data. By putting these declarations into a special file (on UNIX this is usually given the extension of '.h') we can then use this with the 'include' to ensure that all of the files will be compiled using exactly the same set of declarations.

A very simple example of the use of this with FORTRAN might be to use such a file to hold the details of any COMMON blocks being shared between several independently compiled parts of a large program. Suppose the file 'common.h' contains the following source lines:

```
COMMON /GRAPH/ X(100),Y(100)/ BUFFER / HEAP(40)
COMMON /SWAP/ MATRIX(20,25)
```

If a program contains the statement

```
INCLUDE common.h
```

among its declaration statements, it will pick up the declarations of the COMMON blocks GRAPH, BUFFER and SWAP at that point, just as though those lines were a part of the program.

Note that in this example the language words appear in upper-case letters, as convention and the ANSI standard require, although the *f77* compiler will accept lower-case letters too.

Use of 'undefined'

The 'undefined' option provides a way to overcome the all-too-frequent occurrence of the old FORTRAN bogey which arises from the combination of the implicit typing rules (variable names beginning with a letter in the range I to N are integers, and all others are reals, unless explicitly defined otherwise); and the ability to declare a new variable simply by assigning a value to it. With this pair it is very easy to create a new variable of predefined type by a key-punching slip when entering a program. Detecting the existence and then determining the location of such errors can be very time-consuming.

When the 'undefined' option is specified to the compiler, *f77* will turn off this implicit typing mechanism and flag as an error any reference made to a variable that has not been previously declared at the beginning of the program or subprogram. As anyone who has used an Algol-type language where this feature is standard will know, the extra key-punching time is usually more than offset by the time saved in debugging the program. The use of 'undefined' with *f77* is particularly recommended to any FORTRAN programmer to use as a regular programming practice.

input and output

The input/output facilities of *f77* are fairly conventional, although a few additions are provided to allow the programmer to make fuller use of the UNIX file handling features. By default each program begins execution with logical unit 5 preconnected to the user's keyboard (the **standard input**) and with logical unit 6 preconnected to the user's screen (the **standard output**). Both assume sequential formatted input/output which is the normal FORTRAN default form. Further details about input and output for FORTRAN programs are given in Chapter 7.

6.1.3 *ratfor*

Before FORTRAN 77 appeared and provided the FORTRAN language with some degree of structure, the creators of UNIX had solved the structuring problem by using a pre-processor program. This took in as its source file a file containing a form of structured FORTRAN and produced as its output the equivalent program in standard FORTRAN IV. This *ratfor* pre-processor was itself written in standard FORTRAN IV and proved a highly useful and portable software tool. *ratfor* is still available, but is now mainly used only to maintain existing programs that were developed in the past with its aid. Since so many of its features now appear in the 1977 standard, there is little to be gained in using it for the development of new programs—although it is still the only means of obtaining such structures as 'while' loops and 'switch' statements in FORTRAN.

6.2 Using the compilers

For the rest of this chapter it is assumed that the reader has sufficient knowledge of at least one of the main languages to appreciate the important aspects of compiler use. Since both *cc* and *f77* are used in much the same manner as regards options and parameters, most of the examples will be given for *f77* as FORTRAN is more widely known, and the C compiler *cc* will only be mentioned where significant differences occur in its use.

6.2.1 Running a compiler

This is done much as for any other UNIX utility, by a command of the general form

```
$ f77 {options} <filename1> { <filename2> ..... }
```

or similarly for C:

```
$ cc {options} <filename1> { <filename2> ..... }
```

The principal options are considered in Section 6.2.2 and for the moment we look at the conventions that apply to the filenames that we pass as parameters to the compiler.

In the simplest form, our program is contained entirely in a single source file, say 'myprogram.f' (note the extension '.f' which denotes a FORTRAN source file). Then the command

```
$ f77 myprogram.f
```

will cause the compiler to take this file as its input and generate an **object file** or **intermediate code file** named

```
myprogram.o
```

Note the extension '.o' which denotes an object file. This is then linked together with the standard FORTRAN library routines to produce the final executable file named 'a.out'.

We can give a sequence of filenames, separated by spaces, to the compiler as in the line

```
$ f77 master.f sub1.f sub2.f
```

In this case, each of these files will be compiled in turn, to produce three files of intermediate code, and the link-editor will then link all three of these files together to produce a single 'a.out' file. The case where each of these files is compiled independently at different times and are then put together is considered when we look at compiler options in Section 6.2.2.

The compilers (and *f77* in particular) are very tolerant about the input parameters that they can accept, and will accept a mix of source and intermediate code files in the command line, and handle them correctly to produce a final program. For example, in the command

```
$ f77 master.o sub1.o sub2.f
```

the FORTRAN compiler will compile the contents of 'sub2.f' to produce the new file 'sub2.o' and then pass all three of the '.o' files to the link-editor to use in creating the 'a.out' file. Table 6.1 shows the acceptable extensions that can be used on files input to the C and FORTRAN compilers, and shows that *f77* will even accept files with extension '.c' and correctly pass them to the C compiler! (It also shows that we must include the extension with any filename that we pass to a compiler—there are no defaults assumed by the compiler itself.)

Table 6.1   File extensions for use with *f77* and *cc*

Compiler	Filename extension	Meaning
f77	.f	FORTRAN source file
	.c	C source file
	.r	*ratfor* source file
	.s	assembler source file
	.o	object file
cc	.c	C source file
	.s	assembler source file
	.o	object file

[There is some sound logic behind the acceptance of '.c' files as input to *f77*, because the intermediate code generated is compatible with that from the C compiler. Since for either of the FORTRAN or C languages, a program can be made up from a number of independently compiled modules, it is also possible under UNIX to make it up from a set of modules which are not even written in the same source language. It is not particularly easy to do this, nor is it a practice to be recommended, but on rare occasions it may enable the FORTRAN programmer to call upon facilities that are not usually available within the language. Should this need occur, and our program is then made up of (say) a main routine in the file 'boss.f' and a set of subroutines in the file 'sub1.f', all written in FORTRAN, as well as the file 'sub2.c' containing the subroutines that have been written in C, then the one line

```
$ f77 boss.f sub1.f sub2.c
```

will cause the appropriate compiler to be used to compile each of the source files; and the three files generated ('boss.o', 'sub1.o' and 'sub2.o') will then be passed on to the link-editor.]

Unless we specifically direct otherwise, the compilers will follow a successful compilation sequence by invoking the link-editor *ld*, to combine the object files, add any
necessary library routines and then produce the final executable image file 'a.out'. It is
generally much easier to use *ld* indirectly in this way rather than by calling it directly
since we are then saved the need to specify the details of the appropriate libraries
needed, these being specified within the *f77* and *cc* routines. Unfortunately we cannot
completely forget or ignore the existence of *ld*, because in the event of any errors
occurring during the link-editing sequence, it will of course generate some error
messages—usually because a module or variable is missing. Thus, when we receive error
messages while compiling a program, it may not be immediately obvious whether the
message comes from the compilation part or the link-editor, and this must be determined
from the form and content of the message itself.

6.2.2 Selecting options

While both the C and FORTRAN compilers (and the link-editor) have quite a large set
of options, only a few are likely to be immediately relevant to us for most applications.
Table 6.2 lists some of the more relevant options that are available for *f77, cc* and *ld*.
When calling *ld* via the compilers, any options that are unrecognised by the compiler are
simply passed on to *ld*, which is why they need to use quite different choices of option
letters.

Table 6.2   Useful options for use with *f77* and *cc*

Compiler	Option	Effect
f77 and *cc*	–c	Suppress call to *ld*.
	–O	Call optimiser to optimise object code
	–o filename	Use file 'filename' instead of 'a.out'. for the executable output file.
f77 only	–u	Undefined option—flags as 'undefined' any variables not formally declared in a type statement.
	–C	Add code to provide run-time checks on validity of array subscript values.
	–w	Suppress warning messages.

For either the C or FORTRAN compilers, the most commonly used option is likely to
be '–c'. (Note that options are preceded by a '–' to identify them as such.) This option
suppresses the calling of the link-editor *ld* after the successful compilation of any
modules specified, resulting in the generation of the '.o' files but not of an 'a.out' file. It is
obviously a useful option to be used when individually compiling the component files of a
large program. In developing such a program, we will probably wish to check that each
file in turn is free from syntax errors without needing to compile any other files of the
program. This can be done using the '–c' option, and when all the files have been checked
in this way we can proceed to call up *ld* in the most convenient fashion.

As an example of the use of '–c', consider a program that has been constructed in two
parts which are stored in the files 'main.f' and 'subs.f'. We might wish to check 'main.f'
first, and can do so by entering the command

```
$ f77 -c main.f
```

This will produce a file 'main.o' if no errors are detected. Once this is successful, we can then test 'subs.f' in the same way, and when this compiles successfully too we can combine the whole program using any of the following equivalent commands

```
$ f77 main.o subs.o
$ f77 main.f subs.f
$ f77 main.f subs.o
$ f77 main.o subs.f
```

In the first case the compiler will simply call up *ld* and link the two files together (this is still better than calling *ld* directly ourselves, since the correct libraries will be specified by default). In the second case both source files are recompiled and then the object files are linked; this is really the best form to use as a regular practice, because compilers are generally fast and the slight overhead in recompilation ensures that no changes made since the last compilation have been missed. In the third and fourth cases, one file is recompiled and the other accepted in compiled form to pass directly on to *ld*. All four should produce the same result.

The remaining options of Table 6.2 are only necessary for particular cases, some of which will be considered later. The optimising option '–O' may be useful for these programs involved in extensive number-crunching work, but is often better used after the program has been debugged and is working rather than during development and testing.

6.2.3   Files generated during compilation

As already described, a successful compilation will result in the generation of a '.o' file corresponding to each input source file, and the link-editor phase will produce an executable 'a.out' file. The '.o' files contain the set of machine-level instructions that the compiler has generated to represent the original source-level statements, but with any references to library routines or missing variables and procedures left marked, so that the link-editor can finish resolving these as a part of its task.

The UNIX compilers and the assembler do not produce any other files. In particular they do not produce listing files or map files. This is very much in keeping with the UNIX philosophy of each program performing a single task—in this case, compilation. In practice the absence of any listing files does little more than show that these are not really necessary, since a line-numbered listing of the original source file is quite adequate for debugging and testing of a program. For other information such as symbol tables, a separate utility program must be used, as described in Section 6.2.4.

6.2.4   Other utility programs used in compilation

This sub-heading is rather inaccurate, since these utilities can be used at any time and are not really a part of the compilation process itself. However, they are normally used when constructing programs and are very much associated with compiler use.

The utility program *nm* can be used to produce a **symbol table** from the information stored within the '.o' file and also, if necessary, from the 'a.out' file. The latter is sometimes useful for debugging purposes and occasionally for analysis of the program structure and size.

The *size* utility prints out the number of bytes occupied by the various parts of the compiled program (executable code, data and stack space) and their sum. Where programs become large in terms of the available address space (a particular PDP-11 problem) then this can sometimes be useful to the user who has some knowledge of the segmentation scheme of the PDP-11.

lint has already been mentioned in connection with the use of the C language, and is a useful pre-process to run on any C program before submitting it to *cc* for actual compilation. Even where the syntax of a program is correct, the use of *lint* might aid the detection of omissions or errors by listing such information as the presence of any variables that have been declared and not used.

6.3 Link-editing

Since most of the relevant information about this feature of program construction has already been described in Section 6.2, its actual use will not be further discussed here. Instead, this section simply makes one point about the use of *ld*, and about its inputs.

When using the link-editor *ld* via the compiler commands, one of the particular advantages that was highlighted was that the compiler will organise any necessary references to library files. These library files are formed by including together a number of independently compiled object (intermediate) files in such a way that we can quickly extract a copy of any one of them when required.

It is sometimes useful to gather together a number of our own routines into such a library, either because they are all associated with some particular task or facility, such as using a plotting device, or simply to avoid having to pass long strings of filenames for the link-editor. Such libraries can be constructed using the *ar* (for *ar*chive) utility program. Once such a library has been created, *ar* can also be used to maintain it, adding new routines, replacing old with new where necessary and deleting those no longer needed. Library files are usually distinguished on the file system by having the extension '.a' and are stored in one of the directories /lib or /usr/lib.

6.4 System support facilities

Various library routines can be included in our programs via system calls, to allow programs written in C or FORTRAN to exploit some of the facilities of the UNIX *shell* and environment. While some of the more relevant features will be described in Chapter 7, this section gives a very brief preview of some facets that are relevant to the current topic.

6.4.1 Input and output

For both the FORTRAN and C languages, there are some well-defined packages of input and output routines, those for FORTRAN being properly a part of the language itself. In many ways these are not usually seen as a part of the operating system's support role, although their use does require the program to call upon the system to provide various facilities such as file handling. FORTRAN provides for both formatted and unformatted sequential access to files, as well as for direct access handling methods. The UNIX implementation provides for all of these as standard. Similarly the C language includes routines for the handling of binary or character input and output, as well as for sequential or random access to files and devices where appropriate.

6.4.2   Executive calls

The **C support library** includes routines that allow a program to make requests to the *shell* for various actions, some of them involving the *shell* in running another process and passing back some response (e.g. obtaining the time-of-day). Their use is rather specialist, and is really a system facility rather than a directly language oriented facility; users should obtain the details from the appropriate UNIX manual. The very determined user should also be able to access these from a FORTRAN program, although the value of such an exercise is not immediately apparent.

6.5   The UNIX assembler (PDP-11)

Having admitted to the existence of the UNIX assembler, *as*, it is only fair to describe it in at least a little detail. The obvious contrast to make in doing so is with DEC's own assembler for the PDP-11 range of computers, the Macro-11 assembler—with *as* coming out badly on most counts (but not all). This probably reflects the differing esteem with which assemblers are viewed in the two 'camps'. System programming on UNIX is normally performed using C, and *as* is only used where there is a need to access machine structure, i.e. as a part of the operating system functions. Device driver programs and utility programs are normally coded in C and are hence more easily read and maintained.

Since the principal interest in using *as* might be where a need arises to convert an existing PDP-11 program that has been previously written in Macro-11 so that it will now run under UNIX, it is well to begin with conventions, as these are significantly different. The particular conventions of the Bell Laboratories terminal handler process (which were mentioned in Chapter 3) make the use of the '#' and '@' characters rather inconvenient for programming, as they are used by the terminal handler for 'delete' and 'erase line' respectively. This is unfortunate in view of the wide use of both these characters within the Macro-11 syntax. Table 6.3 shows the main differences between the conventions used by the two assemblers.

Table 6.3   Significant differences between *as* and Macro-11

Function	Macro-11	as
Comment	;	/
Immediate mode	#	$
Indirect mode	@	*

There are also very few **pseudo-instructions** (assembler directives) in *as*, and most are fairly familiar, such as:

```
.byte
.even
.if
.endif
.globl
```

(Note that the period '.' indicates a pseudo-instruction in *as* too.) Others are less familiar, such as:

```
.text
.data
.bss
```

which deal with the segmentation of a program (essentially replacing the '.psect' directive in a rather more limited fashion). Block storage can be allocated by using the form

```
.=.+n
```

where 'n' is the number of bytes by which the position counter should be advanced. There are no pseudo-instructions for block storage allocation.

One feature in which *as* has a definite advantage over Macro-11 is in its handling of local labels. For Macro-11, a local label has the form

```
n$:
```

(e.g. 3$:, 10$:, etc.) with the value of 'n' being a unique number within the scope defined by any two standard labels. So once a value of 'n' has been used it cannot be used again until a standard label has been used. In *as* this is replaced by a system of local labels which simply have the form

```
n:
```

(e.g. 5:, 25:, etc.). When such labels are referenced within the program code it is via the value of 'n', followed by the letter 'b' or 'f' to indicate whether it is to be the next label of that value 'back' or 'forward'. This makes the code much easier to read since the direction of a branching instruction's target label is then immediately established. In addition, a label may itself be re-used at any time without ambiguity. A very simple example of this would be a piece of program such as

```
4:   dec r0          /decrement the count register
     cmp r0,r1        /and compare with contents of register 1
     beq 4b           /loop back if equal
4:   add $4,r1        /add constant 4 to register 1
```

The various system calls to the *shell* that were mentioned in Section 6.4 are also available to assembler programs. However, the interface is not well described anywhere, although the sections of the manual dealing with the calls usually describe the calling protocol. The simple program in Fig. 6.2 shows a very simple example of an assembler program which will run under UNIX—and demonstrates why anyone wishing to learn assembler writing skills might do well to begin elsewhere (or at least with a more simple machine and a more tolerant assembler)! Similarly, while programs written in Macro-11 can be converted to run under UNIX, it may be easier to begin again by re-coding them in C as a better long-term solution.

6.6   Error messages

Error messages generated by the compilers themselves vary from the fairly conversational, providing such details as the original source line number (in *f77*), to the rather

```
/           simple example of an assembler program
/           to try out the Unix version of the PDP11 assembler
/           to assemble this file use the string :-
/
/           as /usr/include/sys.s try.s
/
/
/
start:  clr     r0
        clr     r1
        clr     r2                  /clear the first 3 registers
        mov     $20,r1
        mov     $buffer,r2
        mov     $101,r0             /put ASCII ´A´ in r0
loop:   mov     r0,(r2)+            /set up locations 3000 - 3020
        inc     r0                  /bump to next character each time
        dec     r1                  /decrement counter
        bgt     loop
        clr     r2

        sys creat;name;600          /create the file
        mov     r0,r3               /keep identity of file in r3
        sys write;buffer;20

        mov     r3,r0               /reset identity in r0
        sys close
        clr     r0                  /set null in r0 before exiting
        sys     exit
buffer: .=.+400
name :  <new.dat>                   /set up string containing file name
```

Fig. 6.2 An example program using the Assembler *as*. This example program creates a file named 'new.dat' and writes an alphabetically ordered string of characters to it. Calls to the operating system are preceded by the command 'sys'.

terse (*cc*), and the generally unhelpful (*as*). In compensation for the curtness of *cc* itself though, *lint* gives quite verbose reports of its findings on the user's screen (the volume of these may make the redirection technique described in Chapter 7 rather useful).

A common error message from the link-editor *ld* concerns missing symbols, the missing symbols being listed on the user's screen. The first problem is usually to remember that *ld* is there at all. Having done that, and identified it as the likely source of the error message, the next problem is to identify the missing symbols. Those given may be almost recognisable—but with the odd underscore character '__' added fore and/or aft. Those unrecognised should be ignored at this point since they are generally not genuine errors, but simply reflect the inability of *ld* to complete its task without the symbols that you need to provide yourself. Correct these and the others will generally go away. A simple example of this is shown below. The program in file 'analyse.f' calls a subroutine 'fourier', stored in another file. If we compile the main part, forgetting to include the second file, then we get a string of messages of the form

```
$ f77 analyse.f
analyse.f:
   MAIN:
undefined:
_fourier_
_end
```

The first message are from *f77* which is reporting as it compiles each module within the file; the 'undefined' and the following two labels are generated by *ld*. If we provide the routine 'fourier', then the need for label '_end' will also disappear.

References

1. Kernighan, B W, and Ritchie, D, *The C Programming Language*, Prentice-Hall, 1978.
2. Feldman, S I, and Weinberger, P J, *A Portable FORTRAN 77 Compiler*, UNIX V7.
3. Ritchie, D M, *UNIX Assembler Reference Manual*, UNIX V7.

7
Running programs with the UNIX shell

Keywords

adb; *echo*; redirection; search path; shell program; shell variables; standard error output; standard input; standard output; *test*

7.1 Introduction

Much of the material covered in Chapter 6 assumed that sooner or later we will be writing and running programs of our own, or at least modifying existing programs and running the new versions. To do this we need to be able to construct programs, and also to have some understanding of how they will interact with their environment when they are used and how data can be routed into and out from our program.

This chapter is concerned with this interaction between a process (i.e. the memory image of our program) and its environment, especially in terms of any file handling required. It also provides an introduction to the very important topic of shell programming, introducing some of the facilities that are provided in this very powerful software tool. It is at this point that the special features of UNIX begin to emerge.

7.2 Executable files

Before the UNIX *shell* generates a process by copying the contents of our compiled and linked program file into main memory, it first checks the file to make sure that it possesses the appropriate attribute, i.e. that it is tagged as an **executable** file. The three protection bits that are associated with each file on the system were described in Chapter 4, and the important one in this case is the 'x' attribute. Unless a file has this attribute set for the appropriate class of user, the *shell* will reject any attempts that we make to execute the contents of that file.

Of course, we do not usually get involved in the task of setting this attribute for our executable files, this being done for us by the link-editor *ld* when it generates an 'a.out'-type file. Similarly, if we make a copy of the file, as in

```
$ cp a.out newprog
```

then the attributes of the original file are copied to the new one. This can therefore be used in the same way as the original by entering the command

```
$ newprog
```

(Remember—there is no 'run' command in UNIX.)

Files that have been generated by compiling a program source file are therefore directly machine-readable, i.e. they consist of bit patterns which correspond to instructions belonging to the instruction set of the particular computer's central processor unit (cpu). As well as these files, we may also designate as executable any files which contain a series of *shell* commands. (On other operating systems these are sometimes called by such names as **command files** or **macros**.) While the format of such files is left until later in this chapter, it is worth noting here that such **shell programs**, as these files are called, are run in just the same manner that we run the machine-readable files. It is left for the *shell* to determine which type of file is being used and to process the file accordingly.

This equivalence of all executable files will later prove to be a very useful feature, since it means that we can run any program given to us without needing to know which type of executable file it is.

7.2.1   Finding the file

When we direct the *shell* to run a particular program, by typing in its name (or more correctly, the name of the file in which it is stored), the *shell* must first locate the file. It first searches our own current directory (which may be one of our sub-directories) for an executable file of that name, and if it does not find one, it then searches the other directories that lie on its search path.

The usual search path is a list of only two directories, which have already been mentioned as those that are used to hold utility programs intended for general use, namely:

    /bin   and   /usr/bin

This default search path, or list of other directories to search, is actually a shell variable (remember that the *shell* is actually a process too), and may be changed if required. The sort of situation where we might want to redefine this might be where a group of users share some programs that are local to the group, and are stored in a common directory. Rather than have to specify the full path name of the files each time, it would be easier to change the search path for each member of the group to include this shared directory. In Section 7.7.4 we shall see how this form of tailoring can easily be performed when we log into the system.

7.3   Standard input and standard output

Whenever the *shell* starts a new process running, it connects two data streams to it, on which it performs any necessary file handling initialisation. These two streams are character streams and are connected to the user's keyboard and screen by default. They are known as the **standard input** and the **standard output**.

For programs written in the language C, there are input procedure calls to take their data from the standard input, and output procedure calls that send their output to the standard output. Another set of procedures are used for performing input from and output to other files that may be opened. (The procedures for use with standard input and standard output form a concept that is very similar to the INPUT and OUTPUT streams used with Pascal programs.) For programs written in FORTRAN, calls to read input from logical unit 5 will take data from the standard input by default, while anything that is output to logical unit 6 will be routed to the standard output.

For a very large class of programs, these two data streams may well be sufficient, allowing data to be passed into the program and any results to be output to the user. (Both C and FORTRAN provide facilities enabling programs to access other files too.)

The following sections show particularly why these two streams are often quite enough to allow us to create some very versatile and general-purpose programs.

7.3.1   Redirecting the standard input and standard output

The UNIX *shell* provides a very simple means of redirecting either of these two character streams, so that they can be connected to ordinary UNIX files instead of the user's keyboard and screen when the program is executed. In particular, this redirection is quite invisible to the program. This facility is a very important consequence of the UNIX policy of making the system's interfaces to files and devices quite indistinguishable from one another as far as the process is concerned. As we will see later in this chapter, this facility becomes even more useful when it is coupled with the use of the shell programming facilities.

Despite its central importance to much of the remainder of this text, the redirections are very simple to describe and to use.

Redirecting the standard input
When it is directed to run a process, the *shell* will normally connect the standard input of the process to our keyboard, and will perform the necessary file handling functions to allow us to enter data directly when a request for input is made by the program. To use a pre-prepared file of characters (text) as our input instead of typing it in directly, all that we need to do is to include the string

```
< 'filename'
```

in the command line telling the *shell* to run the program. The character '<' instructs the *shell* to perform its file open functions on the specified file instead of the keyboard, so that the program will now read its standard input from the specified file. As a simple example of this, suppose that we have a program stored in the file 'transform', which reads a set of data values from our keyboard and after duly processing them writes the results of this processing back to our screen. During the preliminary testing of this program, it may be useful if we can keep entering the same test patterns of data in order to check for the correct responses; and so to reduce human errors as well as to ensure consistency of the testing, it would clearly be an aid to have these test patterns stored in various files such as 'test1.dat'. To run our program taking its input from 'test1.dat' we then simply type in the command:

```
$ transform <test1.dat
```

and 'transform' will read its data from 'test1.dat' until either it terminates (because of an error or because the processing is complete) or until it encounters the end-of-file marker in 'test1.dat'—the equivalent of typing in control-Z from the keyboard.

Redirecting the standard output
This is redirected in much the same way that we use with the standard input, with the '>' character being used to tell the *shell* to create a new file and to route the output data to it. For example, the command

```
$ cat file1 >filecopy
```

will copy the contents of 'file1' into the new file 'filecopy' instead of to the screen. If a version of 'filecopy' already exists then it will be replaced by the new version as usual. (We can already see something of the flexibility of this scheme by the way that we have produced a simple equivalent of the 'copy' utility *cp* by this one action.)

For the case of the standard output, we also have a second option available to us, which is to append our output to the end of an existing file rather than creating a new one each time. To do this we use the double character '>>' instead of '>'. An example might be

```
$ cat file2 >>filecopy
```

and this time, provided that 'filecopy' already exists, the contents of the file 'file2' will be added to the end of the existing contents of 'filecopy'. If no file 'filecopy' exists, then the '>>' acts as if it were a '>' and will create a new one.

This facility for appending data to an existing file is particularly useful in building up files from various sources. One use is the maintenance of various forms of 'log' files in which new entries are made at the end of the file whenever the appropriate event occurs, in order to maintain an historical record. With the aid of shell programming this can usually be provided quite easily.

Later in this text we will see many more examples of the use of redirecting the standard input and the standard output, since it enables us to make very wide use of some quite simple single-functioned programs.

Error messages

Some of the routines provided in the various run-time support libraries used by such languages as C and FORTRAN contain internal checking for erroneous situations (e.g. zero division), and will print out error messages on the user's screen if such errors are detected when the process is running. To avoid having these error messages accidentally redirected into a data file, along with the rest of the standard output, the *shell* opens up a third character stream for each process that it runs. This **diagnostic output** is permanently connected to the user's terminal and cannot be redirected in any way. It is conventionally used by the run-time library routines, although users may access it too if they wish, to output their own error messages (for *f77* the **diagnostic logical unit** is logical unit 0; for C programs the **standard error output** is file descriptor 2).

7.4 Using other files for input and output

Besides the standard input and the standard output, for which the system provides all of the necessary file handling protocols, UNIX processes are able to use other files too. The detailed use of these is rather language-dependent and the next few paragraphs outline the cases for the languages C and FORTRAN only.

7.4.1 Using other files with FORTRAN

The default uses for the logical units 0, 5 and 6 have been described in Section 7.3, and of course any of the others may be used for input or output as required. If we read from or write to any other logical unit without first specifying via the 'open' statement the filename required, then the supporting input/output library routines will allocate to it the default filename

```
fort.n
```

where 'n' is the value of that particular logical unit. For example, if a program writes its data to logical unit 1, then this will cause a file named 'fort.1' to be created by the FORTRAN support library routines and used to receive the data; it will also be opened for sequential formatted output. Similarly, if the first use of logical unit 2 is to read data, then the support library will seek for a file 'fort.2' and open it for use if found. Again, the default form of access will be sequential formatted.

Should we prefer to use a specific file for input, or to create a file with a different name, then we must use the FORTRAN **open** statement which has the form

```
open(1,file='rawdata')
```

where the use of this would cause the file 'rawdata' to be used in place of the default filename 'fort.1'. Note too that the filename can include the directory path where appropriate too; for example,

```
open(3,file='datasub/results')
```

This will open the file 'results' in sub-directory 'datasub'. (The open command has various other parameters too, including a 'status return' which should normally be used and tested as a matter of good programming practice.)

A particular point to note about the FORTRAN file handling routines on the UNIX system is that they open an existing file with the current record being the one at the end of the file—so that for input a **rewind** must be performed before any data can be read in, to avoid the first **read** finding the end-of-file marker. For the case of output, if no rewind is performed, then any 'write' statements will append data to the end of an existing file rather than opening a new output file.

7.4.2   Using other files with C

As might be expected, the C language is supported by a whole range of library routines for creating and using files on the UNIX system. Within a C program itself, files other than the standard input and output are referenced via **file pointers**, these being pointers to data items of the type FILE, which is predefined in the C language. Such pointer variables must be declared at the beginning of a program, and can then be attached to any particular file by using the 'fopen' procedure. (C also provides a lower level of access, which rather confusingly involves the use of **file descriptors** rather than file pointers.) Overall this scheme is very similar to using the logical unit numbers of FORTRAN, although it is more flexible in allowing different levels of access to the data within a file. For further details of input and output in the C language, refer to a C programming manual or *The C Programming Language* by Kernighan and Ritchie.

7.5   Run-time errors

When errors occur during the execution of a user's process, they will be intercepted and handled by one of two levels of software, these being

the run-time library routines of the language
the *shell* itself.

Which level is used depends on the severity and type of error (or **exception**) that has occurred and the level of diagnostics that have been provided in the language's run-time support library.

Error messages that are intercepted by the library routines are generally connected with input/output formats, and may involve errors such as the use of data elements of incompatible types. In the case of a language like Pascal there may also be optional checking routines that can be built in to a process to perform such tasks as checking that the index value of an array lies within the legal bounds whenever the array is accessed.

Messages from the library routines will usually try to give some indication of the type of error and its location within the original source program. *f77* is rather good at this, others less so. It is also usual for a process to be terminated when such errors are detected, although not necessarily so since not all such errors have fatal effects.

The error conditions that are handled by the *shell* are usually those that are intercepted by the hardware of the processor itself. Such errors are likely to be inadvertent attempts to access data at memory addresses that lie beyond the block of memory allocated for the process, or where the central processor has encountered a machine-level instruction which it does not recognise, termed an **invalid op-code**. A likely source of the latter type of error is a data overwrite or an error in pointer usage, which may result in the processor trying to execute data instead of instructions. On detecting such an error, the *shell* will abort (**kill**) the process and will copy its final memory image at the point where the error occurred into a file named 'core' in the user's current directory, together with such additional information as the contents of the various registers of the cpu at that point.

Errors that are detected by the processor hardware will generally be harder for the user to cure, since the real cause of the error may not be clearly indicated by what has happened. On the PDP-11 this is not helped by the *shell* only ever providing one error message for all types of error, namely

> Bus error, core dumped

quite regardless of the fact that the processor's hardware has provided the *shell* with at least some indication of the actual type of error that it has intercepted.

While it is possible to extract some information from the file 'core', it does require familiarity with the processor's structure and its instruction set at the machine level. Even for an experienced assembler programmer, there may still be difficulty in relating this back to the original source program if this was in C or FORTRAN (say). Faced with this type of error, systematic use of printing statements to trace the progress of a process may be the best policy and should at least enable the offending section of the program to be identified.

7.6 Debugging tools

For those willing and able to control the execution of their programs at the machine-code level, UNIX provides a very powerful debugging tool, the *adb* utility program. *adb* is really rather a departure from the UNIX philosophy of each software tool doing just one job, and doing it well. *adb* does several jobs and is very far from being a particularly easy program to use. Part of this inconsistency arises from the dual facilities that it provides for the programmer, who can use it to control the running of a process, and also to examine the 'core' file—working with both at the same time if necessary. The resultant complexity of available commands, and of interpreting the results of these, shows how sound the UNIX philosophy is, and how nice it would have been for *adb* to have adhered to it!

Since this text is not intended to cater for those working at the machine level, noting the presence of *adb* will suffice at this point, and would-be users should consult the appropriate UNIX documents.

7.7   Programming the *shell*

The ability to store *shell* commands in a file and then use this file to direct the action of the *shell* has already been mentioned. This major section provides an introduction to the ideas of **shell programming** and the basic mechanisms involved, while leaving some of the more powerful aspects of use to be further developed in Part II where it will form an important means for underpinning the ideas presented there.

Other operating systems often allow the user to create files which contain strings of commands, and while this is the basis of shell programming, it does involve rather more than simply using sequences of commands. Shell programming includes structuring facilities so that the programs may be structured using the basic trio of **sequence**, **selection** and **iteration** (or 'if-then-else', 'case' and 'looping' constructs if you prefer). It also includes the abilities to use redirection of the standard input and the standard output and to couple the standard output of one process into the standard input of another (pipes). Taken together, these facilities provide us with what is effectively a very high-level programming language with existing programs providing the 'functions' and 'subprograms' for this higher level.

Shell programs are created and changed using the text editor *ed* and are ordinary files of characters (text), just like the source files for any other programming language. In their most simple form they just contain a sequence of *shell* commands. (Any UNIX program can be invoked within a shell program, since all that happens when we run a shell program is that the standard input of the *shell* itself is taken from the designated file instead of from the keyboard—a concept that we have recently met for other processes.) Before going any further, it may help to consider a very simple example of a shell program and how we can create and use it.

7.7.1   A simple example of a shell program

The example chosen is really very trivial, but should suffice to show the mechanics of producing a shell program, leaving the more subtle aspects for later.

The example assumes that when we use the utility *ls*, we normally like to get a full listing of our directory (i.e. file attributes, last date of modification, size in bytes, etc.), and to have it ordered by time of last modification rather than the default of alphabetical ordering by filename. To help further, we also want to print out the current time and date on our screens whenever we use *ls* (using the utility program *date* which does just this for us). To create ourselves a shell program to do all this we use the normal text editor *ed*, and create a file called 'dir' (say), into which we enter the two lines

```
date
ls -lt
```

(try doing this). After exiting from the editor we can check the contents of the file 'dir', using *cat* for reassurance if necessary:

```
$ cat dir
```

At this point, only one more action is needed from us before we can go ahead and use our new program, and that is to give the file 'dir' the 'x' attribute so that the *shell* will be willing to run the program. To do this we use the utility *chmod*, and enter the command line

```
$ chmod u+x dir
```

(this gives the user (u) execute permission (+x) for the file 'dir'. We use the symbols '+' to grant a permission and '–' to remove it). We may then run our shell program by typing in its name as usual:

```
$ dir
```

and the *shell* will then read the file 'dir' and execute the commands it finds there until it encounters the end-of-file marker. At this point it will return to taking its input from the keyboard once more, issuing a new user prompt to indicate this.

Note that we need to use *chmod* (*change mode*) only once on a file; any subsequent editing of the file will leave the attributes unchanged.

This example has shown little of the potential that lies in shell programming, although some may be already apparent from the earlier sections of this chapter. However, it does show how easily we can create shell programs. Later examples will show why the term 'programming' is used, since when we use the *shell* in this way we are really treating it as a very high-level interpreter.

An important point to note from the example is that a shell program is used in just the same way as a binary image file generated by the link-editor. Provided that the file that we want to execute has the 'x' attribute then the *shell* will accept it—and determine for itself which type of file it actually is. Some of the normal UNIX utility programs that you use are really shell programs—but there is no way (other than trying to list them) of telling which these are. In this sense UNIX goes much further than many operating systems which offer similar facilities, since these often expect the user to indicate which type of file is being used, perhaps by prefixing the filename with a special symbol. The UNIX form is much more convenient for the user.

We can use the *shell* to tailor our own set of commands like the example above, and this can be helpful if you find some of the utility names hard to remember. Note too that we can also use redirection of standard input and output within the shell programs, and this will be freely used in some of the following examples.

To be able to make full use of our ability to write 'shell programs' in this way, we also need to know how to pass parameters to a shell program, but before examining how this is done it is useful to look at a few of the UNIX utility programs that are included primarily or solely to aid in shell programming.

7.7.2 A few utility programs

While many of the UNIX utility programs such as *cat* are useful on their own and also within shell programs, there is a small group of these that perform tasks that are largely irrelevant when using them directly, and which are specifically included to support the various constructs used in shell programming. Some particularly useful ones are as follows.

at	defers the execution of a process until the specified time-of-day.
sleep	defers the execution of a process for the specified period.
awk	is a powerful pattern scanning and processing language which will be used in some of the examples of Part II.
date	obtains the current date and time-of-day (useful for logging information).
echo	writes its argument (a text string) to the standard output.
expr	is used to manipulate shell variables when we need to perform arithmetic operations. Shell variables are usually treated as strings of characters, whether made up of digits or not.
grep	searches a given file (or files) for a pattern match to the character string given as its argument (this is useful at any time, not just when shell programming).
test	checks the status or existence of a given file, performs matching tests on strings of characters, or compares values of numeric strings.
time	gives the amount of time elapsed, and the proportion used by the cpu, in executing a given command.

By far the most widely used of these is *echo* which is obviously of little use except when shell programming. *echo* can be used to write prompts to the user as well as any error messages that are necessary, and can also be useful when used with the redirection facility in providing items such as headings in logging files. The following simple example shows its use for prompting within a shell program:

```
echo
echo 'set the vdu to page mode'
echo
```

Each call of *echo* causes the characters output to be terminated by a 'newline' unless explicitly overridden by the '–n' option—so that a call of *echo* with no arguments will simply cause a blank line to be generated on the screen. This command sequence will therefore generate a blank line followed by the line of text

```
set the vdu to page mode
```

and then another blank line.

When considering the forms for structuring shell programs we will also quite frequently encounter the use of the *test* utility, as it is often used to establish a condition for a branching or looping construct. Of the others in the list given, *awk* is by far the most addictive (and very useful for many database applications) and *grep* is always a useful tool to use when debugging or maintaining programs.

7.7.3 Passing parameters to shell programs

The example of 'dir' that we have already examined is fine as it stands. However, for many other applications where shell programming would be useful, we also need to be able to specify one or more filenames as parameters. These will generally then be used as parameters for the programs called inside our shell program. The mechanism for passing parameters to shell programs and using them is quite simple, and in turn this extends our programming powers quite considerably.

When we call for a program to be run under the UNIX *shell* and wish to specify parameters which the *shell* is to pass to the program, we enter the command in the form

```
$ progname filename1 filename2 filename3
```

(ignoring the presence of any options at this point). The various parameters of our program, stored in file 'progname', are the files 'filename1', 'filename2' and 'filename3', the names of the parameters being separated either by spaces or by tab characters. If the program 'progname' were actually a shell program, then within this we could access the arguments symbolically by means of the standard shell variables $1 to $n, where n is the number of parameters. In this case we will have three such parameters, which can be accessed using the symbols $1, $2 and $3. Whenever we make a reference to these variables in our shell program, the string corresponding to the actual parameter will be substituted when the program is run.

To make this a bit clearer, consider how we can create our own version of the *cp* (copy) utility using a one-line shell program and the utility *cat*. This can be written as

```
cat $1 >$2
```

If we store this line in a file called 'owncopy', then once we have given it the 'x' attribute we can go ahead and use it as (say)

```
$ owncopy biffo bear
```

in order to make a copy of the contents of file 'biffo' in file 'bear'. (Remember that the contents of any previous file named 'bear' will be lost.) When we run the shell program as above, the string 'biffo' is substituted for any occurrence of '$1', and the string 'bear' for any occurrence of '$2', so that the actual line executed will be

```
cat biffo >bear
```

and therefore *cat* will copy the contents of 'biffo' to the standard output, which in this case has been redirected to file 'bear'.

Besides the shell variables $1, . . . $n, two other shell variables are useful when handling parameters. They are

$* which is the complete argument string, spaces and all, treated as a single line of text (e.g. 'biffo bear' in the above example);

$# which contains the number of parameters actually provided when the program was called.

An important point to note is that any parameters given are passed and handled as strings of characters, i.e. the *shell* is only performing text string substitution. When we later come to consider how to pass numerical values to shell programs, and how they are handled, we shall need some means of converting the character string to the actual numerical value, which is where the program *expr* is particularly useful.

7.7.4 Variables in shell programs

The parameters passed to a shell program are handled in the same way as any other variables are handled within a shell program. We may create new local variables within such a program simply by reference to them, rather as with FORTRAN, without having to first declare them. They are all treated as character strings—hence no 'typing' of variables. Particular variables that are already being used by the *shell* include those used to define the search path for finding executable files, the identity of the home directory (i.e. the one that we are currently logged into), and the primary and secondary prompts which we met in Chapter 3. To use the value of any of these default variables in an expression (their names being HOME, PATH, PS1 and PS2 respectively), we must precede their name with the '$' character—hence $HOME, $PATH, $PS1 and $PS2. (We have already met this with the positional parameter variables themselves, as well as the parameter count '#', which we met as '$#' in Section 7.7.3.) The normal *shell* wildcard substitutions (*, ?, [ ]) can also be used within shell programs.

7.7.5   The file '.profile'

One of the initial tasks of the *shell*, following a login by the user, is to search the home directory for a file named '.profile'. If such a file is found, then the *shell* will attempt to execute it as a shell program, before prompting the user for commands.

The idea of this was briefly mentioned in Section 3.9, and we are now in a better position to see how it can be used to create a personalised environment. At the most elementary, it need do no more than be a one-line program to change the primary prompt, as in:

```
PS1='unix>'
```

which will cause the *shell* to prompt us with the strong 'unix>' each time instead of the '$' symbol. As we become more fluent with the use of UNIX, and with using the shell and other utility programs, then we are likely to find many more ways of using the '.profile' file. Such possibilities might include maintaining a diary file so that the day's events can be printed out when we first log in: keeping a record of our login times, printing out results from any data analyses made overnight, etc. Everyone is likely to have their own ideas of what is useful, and most of it can be managed with very simple code. In Part II we shall encounter a few more ideas for this.

7.7.6   Structured programming with the *shell*

The very simple example of 'dir' showed how we can create a shell program which consisted of a **sequence** of shell commands. This alone is quite sufficient for many purposes and enables us to perform some useful tasks—for example, with the '.profile' file. However, to be able to perform true programming with the *shell*, we need two other forms of structuring, namely **selection** and **iteration**, and the various forms that these can take are briefly introduced in the rest of this section, together with some examples of their use.

Selection

In a high-level programming language, we usually expect to have two forms of 'select' facility provided for our use, typified by the 'if-then-else' construct and the 'case' construct. The first provides for making simple two-way (binary) branches in the flow of control, while the second allows for the multiple choice routing that is sometimes needed. FORTRAN programmers will be aware that FORTRAN acquired the former with the 1977 standard, but still lacks a very adequate 'case' structure, having to make do with the rather unsatisfactory assigned and computed GOTO statements. The *shell* provides both forms of 'select'; with the 'if' there is even an 'elseif' option, although the actual syntax is 'elif'. The *shell* needs to be able to establish some condition which can be used to determine which route is to be used. To see how this works, we first examine the 'if-then-else' facility.

The if-then-else construct

The condition used to determine whether we use the 'then' route or the 'else' route is a status that is returned to the *shell* as a result of executing the sequence of commands that form the 'if' condition. To understand this more clearly, we must first see what is meant by the concept of an exit status.

Whenever a process that has been running under the UNIX *shell* terminates, either because it has reached its end or because it has been terminated by some outside agency (the user) or an error, a **status value** is returned to the process which caused it to be run. This process is normally the *shell* itself (not invariably so though, since processes can themselves cause other 'child' processes to be run). This status value is an integer number whose value indicates the reason why the process terminated. Normal termination is indicated by the status value being zero. We need not concern ourselves with the non-zero values, other than to note that any other form of termination of a process will result in a non-zero status value, but this obviously provides something which can be tested by the *shell*—and hence which can be used as the appropriate condition for the 'if' statement.

The full formal form for the 'if' statement is

```
if list then list { else list } fi
```

The 'if' statement is terminated by the characters 'fi', i.e. 'if' reversed. (Note that to fit it all on to one line in this way would actually require that we use the appropriate *shell* syntax to separate the various parts, since the *shell* normally accepts only one command per line.)

The term *list* in the above can potentially be quite a complex object. It is defined as a sequence of one or more **pipelines**, where each pipeline is itself a sequence of processes, with the standard output of each being connected to the 'standard input' of the next process. (To make this clearer, the *shell* provides a special symbol, '|', to indicate such a pipe, of which we will see more in Part II.)

For our current needs, the list following the 'if' need only be one process, and the one that is most commonly used is the *test* utility. This can be used for performing various forms of test and comparison, which are chiefly of the general forms:

(i)   to make various checks on the status of a file;
(ii) to perform comparisons between strings of characters.

The particular action required in each case is selected by using the appropriate option. Some examples are:

−**r** 'file'   which returns zero status value if the file exists and is readable;
−**f** 'file'   which returns zero status value if the file exists and is not a directory;
−**z** 'sl'   which returns zero status if the string of characters 'sl' is of zero length;

and so on.

Whenever the status value returned from running a process such as *test* is zero, the statements following the 'then' statement (the **then clause**) will be obeyed by the *shell*. If not, then should an 'else' statement be provided, the *shell* will obey the commands making up the **else clause**. If no 'else' clause is provided, the whole 'if' statement is by-passed completely. (Note that although the 'else' clause is optional, there must always be a 'then' clause following an 'if'.)

Since this all sounds rather complicated, some examples are clearly required at this point, and the following should help to illustrate the points just made.

Example 1   Consider a 'compile' command that first checks that the file exists:

```
if test -r $1.c
then cc -c $1.c
else echo 'file not found'
fi
```

will cause the command

```
$ compile patternmatch
```

to use *test* to check for the existence of file 'patternmatch.c' in the current directory. If it is found, the 'then' clause will be used and the C compiler *cc* will be used to compile the file. If the file cannot be found, then the status value returned will be non-zero and the 'else' clause will be used, causing the message

```
file not found
```

to be printed on the user's terminal. As a useful exercise, try using this with the compiler that you prefer, and then change the 'else' clause additionally to echo the name of the file that it has been unable to locate.

Example 2   We can easily extend this example to be rather more flexible, by adding a check to ensure that one (and only one) parameter has been passed when 'compile' was invoked at the terminal. We can use the '#' variable that gives us the number of parameters. For example,

```
if test $# -eq 1
then
     if test -r $1.c
     then cc -c $1.c
     else echo 'file not found'
     fi
else echo 'filename missing or more then one filename'
fi
```

Here the option '-eq' used with *test* will cause it to check that the variable '#' has a value equal to 1, and hence that one parameter was passed. Other options include -ne, -le, -lt, -ge and -gt. Note that here the character strings are evaluated for their actual numerical value, which is then used in the comparison. (Note too that the indentation used in here is purely to aid readability; it is good practice, but is not required by the *shell* itself.)

These two little shell programs are quite simple, but demonstrate that even in so simple a form we can use the structuring to enable us to tailor some useful utility programs of our own, to fit particular tasks that we are undertaking or for more general use.

One point about using structuring concerns the syntax, and can easily lead to errors on first trying to use this facility. The *shell* will normally expect one command per line, and considers the 'return' or 'newline' character to be the terminator of a command. To place more than one command on a line we must use a terminating symbol (actually the ';'). The 'if', 'then' and 'else' are all considered to be separate commands, and so must appear on separate lines unless we specifically separate them with the';' character—this is rather unlike most high-level programming languages.

The 'case' statement

This is less involved than the 'if-then-else', but just as useful. Rather than testing status values to determine which route through the statement to take, the 'case' matches strings of characters for specific patterns. A simple example may help at this point.

Consider a more general form of the 'compile' program that we wrote earlier, but now we allow the file extension character to determine which compiler is invoked. In this example, we use the C, FORTRAN and Pascal (*pc*) compilers to compile files with filenames ending in '.c', '.f' and '.p' respectively.

```
if test $# -eq 1
then
    case $1 in
        *.c) cc -c $1
                echo 'C compilation complete' ;;
        *.f) f77 -c $1
                echo 'FORTRAN compilation complete' ;;
        *.p) pc -C $1
                echo 'Pascal compilation complete' ;;
        *) echo 'unrecognised file extension' ;;
    esac
else echo 'filename missing or more than one filename'
fi
```

Several points about the form of 'case' follow from this.

(i)   As with 'if' and 'fi', we denote the end of 'case' by using the word 'esac' (i.e. reversing the letters).

(ii) We use ';;' to denote the end of a particular branch (which may contain several lines of commands, or even further nested structuring).

(iii) Since we can use '*' to denote 'any string' (remember), we can also provide a catch-all option that will match any patterns left over by using '*' on its own. Of course, this must be the last pattern in the list!

By now you may be ready to try implementing a few ideas of your own.

Iteration

Besides provision for selection, we expect a high-level language to provide us with some form of looping through a sequence of statements, namely **iteration**. While FORTRAN has only the 'DO' loop, many languages offer such structures as 'for' (similar to 'DO'), 'while' and 'repeat-until' to give greater flexibility to express the programmer's ideas. The first two of these, 'for' and 'while', are also available in the *shell* and are sufficient for most needs. (The 'repeat-until' of languages such as Pascal differs only from 'while' in that whereas 'while' applies the condition test at the beginning of the loop, 'repeat-until' applies it at the end, and therefore control always passes through the loop at least once.)

We will not cover these two in the same depth as was applied to 'if' and 'case', since the style of use is very similar, but will confine ourselves to a brief description of each plus an example of use.

The 'for' statement

This is used to transfer control through a sequence of statements for a given number of passes. There is an associated **index variable** which is used to count the passes and identify them. The 'for' is very similar to the 'case' in that the control variable is taken to be a string of characters rather than a number, and hence the 'for' statement also has to supply a list of values that this index will take in turn.

The general form that the 'for' loop takes is:

```
for name { in wordlist } do statementlist done
```

(Note the 'done' rather than 'rof' to terminate the 'for'; selection and iteration have slightly inconsistent style here.) If the 'in wordlist' is omitted, then the default is to execute the loop once for each positional parameter in turn. This is such a common requirement when using 'for' that, rather than having to express it specifically, it has been made the default list.

As an example, we can use this to make our last version of 'compile' even more powerful, by allowing it to be used with a string of filenames rather than just the one argument. We simply create a new file 'build', which contains

```
for i do
    compile $i
done
```

(Note here that the 'do' can appear on the same line as the 'for' when there is no 'in wordlist', although it may be better to get into the habit of always using the ';' or always putting statements on a new line.)

This example is a reminder that we can call any program from within a shell program—including other shell programs. This can aid us in building up our set of software tools in a step-by-step manner.

Instead of having to enter

```
$ compile prog1.c
$ compile prog2.f
```

we can now simply enter the single command

```
$ build prog1.c prog2.f
```

The 'while' statement

The 'while' statement is very similar to the 'if' statement in its syntax, and has the general form:

```
while list { do list } done
```

(Again, note the use of 'done' for the looping statements.)

As with the 'if' statement, the 'while' tests a numeric status value for its control list, and so the control value is usually provided by the use of *test* in just the same way. (Essentially, the only difference between 'if' and 'while' is that in the latter case control keeps returning to the 'while' until the condition fails.) The form:

```
while test -n $i
do
   ....
done
```

will perform the loop for each non-zero argument of the call, which in this case is equivalent to

```
for i
do
   ....
done
```

There is a further form of 'while', called 'until', which reverses the terminating condition. A useful time to use this is when we do not want to perform some action until a condition is satisfied, e.g. to run a program until another program has produced a data file for its use. Using 'until' together with the *sleep* process allows us to keep testing until the condition is true, as in the example:

```
until test -f 'filename'
do sleep 300
done
```

7.7.7 Interactive use of shell programming

So far we have concentrated on the idea of shell programs using these structures of the *shell*, but a useful point about shell programming is that we can use these features interactively too. This can be particularly useful for testing out some of our ideas, since we can type in the commands interactively as we would any other *shell* commands. This is not really surprising, since shell programs are read on the *shell*'s standard input and the *shell* itself does not differentiate between the different forms of source.

When we type in a structured command to the *shell*, it will recognise this, and if the syntax is not complete, the *shell* will keep prompting us with the secondary prompt symbol for more lines until the statement is complete. A simple example would be

```
$ for i in 1 2 3
> do
> sleep 10
> echo 'next pass'
> done
```

This will cause the shell to keep suspending itself for the set period (10 seconds), and printing the message

```
next pass
```

until the count of three arguments is complete. (In this case the actual values of the arguments are quite irrelevant.)

The 'until' form can be particularly useful here, in conjunction with the option of being able to run more than one process from the terminal. Normally when we enter a command to run a program, we do not get another prompt from the *shell* until the process has completed. If we terminate the command line with the '&' character before 'return', then the shell will set the process running, print out its **process identity** value, and return to the user with a prompt again, without waiting for the process to terminate. With 'until' we then have a useful method of having a second process synchronise itself with the first, without our necessarily having to render our terminal inactive until the two have completed. There is a limit to this: if we run too many processes from one terminal then the response to our further commands will suffer accordingly.

7.7.8   Efficiency aspects of shell programming

To anyone who learnt their programming in the days when the efficiency of a program was a critical factor (encouraged by limitations of machine power and by the scheduling algorithms usually applied to batch streams, which penalised long-running programs quite heavily), the idea of shell programming is likely to suggest that the results are likely to be slow and inefficient in terms of machine use. For two reasons, this is generally not so. These are as follows.

(i)   The *shell* is very efficient in scheduling and loading processes into memory, partly due to the very simple scheduling algorithm.
(ii) There is generally adequate machine power available for these overheads in an interactive system, particularly with the latest generation of processors.

There are obvious limits to these points, but to quite a complex degree of structuring the limitations of shell programming are not too severe and are more than countered by the ease and speed that they confer on program development. Shell programming offers an excellent method for prototyping ideas, allowing potential users to try out a design and to make suggestions for improvement, and providing considerable ease in making any changes that are found necessary. Where the overheads are felt to have become too severe, the shell program can then serve as the design basis for a more engineered version produced in one of the high-level languages—which will generally have sufficiently powerful system interfaces to allow the ideas to be directly conveyed from the shell program to the compiled version.

References

1. Bourne, S R, *Programming the UNIX Shell*, UNIX V7.
2. Bourne, S R, *The UNIX System*, Addison-Wesley, 1982.

8

UNIX under another name

8.1 Introduction

At the beginning of this book, it was mentioned that legal issues originally complicated the marketing of UNIX by its originators, Bell Laboratories. Hence its initial use was largely confined to Bell Laboratories themselves, and to bodies such as universities and colleges where the users were likely to possess sufficient skill and motivation to maintain an unsupported operating system. This situation, and the obvious attractions of using a system such as UNIX, inevitably led a number of system suppliers and software houses to try to close the gap, and to make some form of UNIX-like operating system available to a wider market, with the form of software support servicing that a commercial user requires. So far this form of provision has tended to take two forms, as follows.

(i) Marketing (with support) what is essentially the UNIX operating system, usually retargetted on to another processor (i.e. a redirection of the Bell Laboratories code on to another machine, largely by the use of such facilities as the portable C compiler, since most of the UNIX code is written in C). However, human nature being as it is, many enhancements have been included on the way; and equally, many of the bugs have been ironed out to meet commercial standards.
(ii) Marketing, with support, a rewrite of UNIX (i.e. the external appearance of the operating system is the same as that of UNIX, but its internal workings and structures may differ significantly).

Correctly speaking, the first group *are* UNIX operating systems, being based on the original Bell Laboratories code, while the second group are 'UNIX-like', although this difference can be rather blurred by the presence of any enhancements that the first group may possess.

This chapter provides a very short overview of the significant features of three of the many systems that are now commercially available, and which come under the above headings. The systems described are: ZEUS, XENIX and Idris. The text tries to indicate any major areas in which these may differ or be enhanced when compared with UNIX V7 as described here.

These particular three operating systems have been selected because they are used quite widely and are good examples of the points made above, and because information about them is readily available.

Although it might seem out of place in a book that is concerned with how the user can make the most out of using UNIX, rather than with 'how UNIX works', this chapter is nonetheless very relevant to the theme of the whole book—in that it indicates how widely the software tools that have been described may be available on other systems, and, from the enhancements preferred, what points about UNIX other system designers feel to be inadequate in any way. The coverage of the three systems has been very much restricted to what were felt to be the most relevant features, and for each system in turn the following sections describe any particular differences with UNIX V7 and how it supports any significant changes in the following items:

  (i)   terminal interface conventions;
 (ii)   filestore structures;
(iii)   text editing facilities;
 (iv)   support for shell programming;
  (v)   common file handling utility programs, i.e. *cat, ls, rm, mv, cp, grep,* etc.;
 (vi)   the ability to call to the *shell* for executive support features from a program;
(vii)   the main programming languages supported;
(viii)   any particular features that are available to support software engineering practices, particularly for the management of software;
 (ix)   the ease with which the user can add new device driver software in order to be able to use any special devices available to them. (System generation for many of these systems is rather better than for UNIX V7, where available, although many systems are supplied ready configured and users may be unable to reconfigure for themselves.)

8.2   The ZEUS operating system

This operating system is not a rewrite, but is genuine UNIX System V redirected on to the Zilog Z8001 central processor unit, although inevitably some enhancements have been included. (UNIX System V is really a development of UNIX V7. It is upwards compatible and includes some tools such as SCCS—of which more later—which are supported on UNIX V7 but not issued as a part of it.) ZEUS is supplied by Zilog (Exxon) for their 'System 8000', a multi-user system based on the Z8001. To emphasise that ZEUS is a UNIX V7 (or System V) system, Zilog make the claim that any program written in C, COBOL or Pascal that will run under UNIX V7 (or System V) will run under ZEUS after being recompiled on the ZEUS system.

8.2.1   Enhancements

There is a screen editor program, *vi*, in addition to the standard text editor *ed*. Some enhancements have been provided in the *shell* too, and many of the utilities are based upon the widely used variants of the basic UNIX utilities that are issued by the University of California at Berkeley (UCB).

   The most significant enhancement that ZEUS provides is in the area of file handling, with the inclusion of a set of **access control modes**. Under UNIX V7 there are no facilities provided which will allow the user to direct the system that it is to prevent two processes from simultaneously accessing and updating a file. When using ZEUS, besides being able to open a file as normal for reading and writing, the user may also specify what access to the file is permitted to other users while it is open. There are three modes of access that can be granted to processes other than the one that first accesses the file—'shared', 'read-only' or 'exclusive'. Once a process has claimed a file, others can only access it using the permitted forms until the first process releases the file by closing it. The forms of access permitted for these modes are:

   shared mode   any other process may access the file;

read-only mode   any process may access the file in order to read from it, but none other than the owner may write to it;

exclusive mode   no other process may access the file at all.

The 'shared' mode corresponds to the normal UNIX V7 situation, while the 'read-only' and 'exclusive' modes are new states. The provision of these effectively adds a scheme of semaphores which control access that processes may have to a file. These modes are selected by setting two of the bits that are normally unused in the flag parameter used when a file is opened via the standard system calls. Since the 'shared' mode corresponds to setting no bits additional to the normal UNIX V7 format, the system is able to maintain the compatibility with UNIX V7 that is so important.

8.2.2 Significant features of ZEUS

A list of the features considered as being of particular interest was given in Section 8.1, and are described below only where ZEUS differs from UNIX V7. The items are numbered as in Section 8.1.

  (i) Terminal handling. This is essentially the version from the University of California at Berkeley, which does differ from that described in Chapter 3, although none of the differences should cause difficulties for the user.

 (ii) The file system. The only significant difference has already been described in Section 8.2.1.

(iii) Text editing facilities. *vi* has already been mentioned, and will work with most VDUs which possess an addressable cursor facility. This form of text editor is especially attractive when preparing documentation files.

(vii) Languages. As with UNIX V7 there are several available, including C, FORTRAN and Pascal as well as various versions of COBOL. The language PLZ as used with the Zilog processors is also included.

 (ix) A manual is provided to guide the would-be writer of device driver software.

There should be very little that would enable a user to distinguish between UNIX V7 and ZEUS when sitting at a terminal, and the particular enhancements may be utilised or ignored as desired.

8.3 The XENIX operating system

XENIX is again a UNIX System V system (i.e. UNIX V7 for our purposes), and is supported by Microsoft on a range of 16-bit processors (PDP-11, LSI-11, Z8000, Intel 8086, Motorola MC68000). The object in producing XENIX was to provide a well-supported UNIX V7 operating system on a range of popular processors, and the producers emphasise that all users of XENIX are ultimately licenced by AT & T (the parent company of Bell Laboratories).

    Since XENIX is supported on the PDP-11 range of computers, which is the base system for UNIX V7, it is worth looking briefly at how XENIX and UNIX differ. The significant difference (apart from the commercial support), is that XENIX has incorporated a scheme which allows for more use of memory overlays on the medium models of the PDP-11 range (i.e. those that do support the virtual memory hardware, but do not have the separate i & d space facility; see Chapter 13). Using this, the smaller machines can support multi-user operation and also run some of the larger utility programs. As examples, the *lint* and *f*77 utility programs normally require the provision of separate i & d space due to their large size.

8.3.1   Significant features of XENIX

Again, this section only features those topics from the list of Section 8.1 that have been enhanced or extended in any way.

  (i)   The terminal handler. The basic form is that of the Bell Laboratories version, though in the UK a version more akin to that described in Chapter 3 is available. Users can select the preferred form.

 (iii)   Text editing. While *ed* is provided as standard, other text editors are available as part of some of the separately supported packages that can run on XENIX, and these include screen editing facilities.

 (vi)   System calls. The form used is that of UNIX V7, although additional calls have been incorporated in the interface to the *shell* in order to allow a specialist user to make custom calls to the additional software packages that are available.

(viii)   Software engineering facilities are largely those of UNIX V7, although the Source Code Control System (SCCS), and an extended version of the *make* utility are available as additional packages. (The use of SCCS and *make* are covered in Part II.) In addition, XENIX supports such additional packages as word processing and relational database software, together with others more directly related to business or scientific use.

 (ix)   Documentation and examples are provided for the use of those who want to add their own device drivers. As an addition to that, the user manuals have also been rewritten to aid the less 'expert' user!

Again, the user should be unable to discern any significant differences from using UNIX V7 when using XENIX, since enhancements are largely supplied in the form of additional software packages, or lie within the realm of the more advanced system programmer.

8.4   The Idris operating system

Idris is a rather different example to the other two operating systems described in this chapter, in that it is internally a rewrite of UNIX (i.e. a 'look-alike'), and also in that it is based on the sixth edition of UNIX (V6), rather than the seventh. (At the time it was written, UNIX V6 was the current version.)

Idris is a product of Whitesmiths Inc. of New York, and was produced to implement the functionality of UNIX without using any of the original code. This re-implementation of UNIX was based upon a new portable version of the C compiler. This version was designed to be highly portable, and is the means by which Idris has been implemented on the PDP-11 family, and also on the Intel 8080/Zilog Z80 pair of processors, the Intel 8086, the VAX11 and the Motorola MC68000.

For the user of UNIX V7, the chief subject of interest is therefore to establish what significant differences exist between UNIX V6 (as *per* Idris) and UNIX V7. Section 8.4.1 gives a summary of these differences, based on the topics of Section 8.1.

8.4.1 Major features of Idris

Obviously the UNIX philosophy and general style were features of V6 as much as of V7 (the terseness of style seems to have been established at a very early point!). This section is chiefly concerned with the largely, but not wholly, superficial interfacing points that affect the user at his terminal.

(i) The terminal interface. This uses the Bell conventions (i.e. '@' to delete a line, 'rubout' to break into an executing process, etc.), although as they are variables they can be changed by recompiling the kernel code. The default prompt from the *shell* is the '%' rather than the '$'.

(ii) The filestore. The V6 structure is internally different to that of V7 (the i-nodes have a different structure). Filenames, the format for describing chains of directories in specifying a file, and directory creation (*mkdir*), are all the same, as are the conventions for the redirection of standard input and standard output.

(iii) Text editing. The *e* editor is largely similar to *ed* in its basic features and commands, although it offers a secondary prompt '>', and also a third level of prompting for the 'a', 'i', and 'c' commands by using the line number as a prompt. At the level of use described in Chapter 5, users should find little difficulty in adapting themselves to the use of *e*.

(iv) Shell programming. This is significantly different to the form available in V7 in that it is largely restricted to the use of sequences of commands. There is a form of 'logical if', but otherwise no structuring, and even this has only a 'then' clause. Most of the utilities such as *echo* and *test* are there, although the option flags may differ. Shell variables must have names of only one letter. This is definitely one area where the user can see the difference.

(v) File handling utilities. *ls, cat, rm, mv, cp, cd*, etc. are all there and recognisable, although some of the options and option letters will differ from those used with V7. No differences for straightforward use though.

(vi) Calls to the *shell*. There are some differences, which may include the presence or absence of particular system calls, and possibly of the data types used for the parameters of these. This is another area in which to expect some differences, but mainly for the system programmer. However, note that the input/output calls used for C differ from those used on V7, and as described in *The C Programming Language* by Kernighan and Ritchie.

(vii) Languages supported. Whitesmiths can provide C and Pascal compilers, and the Microsoft CIS COBOL is also available. There are various C and Pascal cross-compilers and even cross-assemblers too!

(ix) Device drivers. The Idris system is supplied in binary form, but the source code for the device drivers is included in this so that the would-be writer of device drivers has some examples to use (essential). A guide for creating these for the PDP-11 is provided with the documentation, and the system interface is covered in the manuals.

Overall, for most users the use of Idris would represent a 'reduced' form of UNIX V7, with the main effects only emerging for more ambitious applications as user skills develop, e.g. the limited shell programming facilities.

8.5 Summary

This chapter was included to close Part I of the text by demonstrating how the current generation of UNIX V7 systems and 'look-alikes' differ. Given that UNIX is becoming increasingly seen as a portable operating system—and hence as a form of standard by which to measure others—it is tempting to compare it with the FORTRAN language which pioneered portability for programming. The variations between the versions described are no greater than those that occur between the versions of FORTRAN provided by different computer manufacturers, although perhaps the Idris/V7 comparison is more an analogy with the FORTRAN IV and FORTRAN 77 difference in terms of the level of structuring. One hesitates to draw the analogy with FORTRAN any further: this exercise is left for the reader to pursue.

Part II

Part I of the text should have given an idea of the 'flavour' of the UNIX operating system, while concentrating on introducing the UNIX methods of providing those basic facilities that are to be expected from a practical operating system.

Part II shows some ways in which the features of the UNIX system can be used to tackle the most common classes of task that confront the programmer and the software engineer, whatever their basic discipline. Each chapter takes a problem-oriented approach, seeking to show how UNIX can be used to support what are seen as practical engineering techniques for solving problems.

Chapters 9 and 10 introduce the fundamentals, i.e. the methodologies that underlie the tasks of designing and producing a program that is correct, reliable and maintainable, as well as its supporting documentation. They are tasks that UNIX is very well equipped to support, as the examples will show. The remaining two chapters cover rather more general aspects of problem solving; Chapter 11 is concerned with the facilities for supporting and managing larger programming projects, while Chapter 12 introduces some other UNIX facilities that will become more useful to the programmer as his experience with using UNIX increases.

9
Developing and maintaining programs with UNIX

9.1 Introduction

This chapter and those which follow are partly, but not wholly, concerned with the actual use of UNIX features and software tools. To use UNIX effectively there is a need to combine these facilities with a due regard for such factors as good program structure and design—and to see how the choice of good programming practices can enable the programmer to make a full and effective use of UNIX.

The examples given have been selected on the assumption that a good programmer will not be designing, coding or making significant changes to his programs 'on the fly', during a session at a UNIX terminal. The ability to redirect standard output to files that is described in Chapter 7 makes it particularly easy for the programmer to store output and to list it on a printer for a thorough analysis at the desk. It is generally assumed that no programmer would ever consider doing otherwise! These points about practices are important, for while UNIX is a good servant in the hands of those who wish to engineer their programs in a methodical manner, it is also a two-edged weapon in the hands of the 'terminal cowboy' who prefers to dabble and patch using intuition rather than logic! This chapter is long, because it is concerned with making use of UNIX to perform a number of tasks that are important to all programmers, namely developing, testing and maintaining programs. The programs themselves may be concerned with almost any area of work, but the techniques of programming remain much the same. The examples are taken mainly from the scientific fields, purely because at present these tend to make up the bulk of UNIX applications. They are also more familiar to the author!

Sections 9.1.1 to 9.1.3 provide a short introduction and background for the main themes that will be developed in the rest of this chapter, and the manner in which they will be tackled.

9.1.1 Developing new programs

It is probably true to say that we rarely develop a program that is wholly new, in the sense that we will normally be using at least some techniques and constructs that we have used in other programs. Very often a program that we are producing will be a variant of a type of program that we have written before, so that at least some of the likely problems—and their possible solutions—will be familiar. In addition to that, most programmers will try to use tried and tested existing subprograms or available library routines where possible in order to leave themselves free to concentrate on the new parts of the program.

The practices of software engineering, which will influence the form of Part II very widely, encourage the programmer in this use of tested and proven modules. There is little point in wasting time and effort in 're-inventing the wheel' by writing a new 'sort' function (say) when we might already have a choice between three well-tested ones. The ideas on shell programming developed in Chapter 7 show that UNIX takes a very broad view of what constitutes a program module, and the ways in which this idea of re-usability can be combined with shell programming are considered in more depth in this chapter.

Not all of the features of UNIX are documented in the style and level of detail that one would prefer to have, especially during the learning phase when the conventions and terminology may not be so familiar. With this point in mind, the practice of writing test programs is highly recommended. If you are unsure of how a feature works, or is to be used, then write a very simple program in order to try the feature out in isolation, so that its effects are not masked by other factors within the program. Most programmers are familiar with the idea of writing a 'hello' program when learning a new programming language (Figs 9.1 to 9.4 show examples of such a program for the C, FORTRAN and Pascal languages, as well as for the *shell*). With some of the more powerful UNIX features it is well worth spending the time to write an equivalent program, as a part of the learning process.

```
/*  an example of a 'hello' program in C  */

main()
{
    printf("hello\n");
}
```

Fig. 9.1   A 'hello' program in C

```
c    example of a 'hello' program for f77
c
      write(6,100)
      stop
c
  100 format(x,'hello')
      end
```

Fig. 9.2   A 'hello' program in FORTRAN

```
(*  example of a 'hello' program in Pascal   *)

PROGRAM hello(OUTPUT);
BEGIN
    WRITELN('hello');
END. (* hello *)
```

Fig. 9.3   A 'hello' program in Pascal

```
: example of a 'hello' program for the shell
:
echo 'hello'
```

Fig. 9.4   A 'hello' program using the shell

9.1.2   Maintaining programs

The term **maintenance** really includes two separate categories of task, although neither are necessarily very popular with programmers. One of them is to maintain (in the sense of modify or correct) software which we have ourselves produced, although not necessarily as an individual, since we may program as a member of a group or team. The second is to convert a program that has been running on another operating system (or another version of UNIX) in order to run it under UNIX V7. The two categories involve a number of very different issues and techniques, although there are also practices that are useful to both. The first category is partly concerned with the issues of design methods and design documentation—both of which are pursued a little further in the text —while the latter is much more concerned with the detective work of obtaining an understanding of an unfamiliar program, and probably offers the larger intellectual challenge to the programmer.

One small consolation for the programmer faced with the second task is the thought that effecting it in reverse might be far worse—if only because the facilities of UNIX make it possible to construct programs in many varied forms, some of which would be difficult to emulate successfully on any other operating system.

9.1.3   The software lifecycle

One of the ideas generally associated with the practices of software engineering is that of the **software lifecycle**. This concept attempts to identify the progress or history of a program, of any size, from the raising of the initial requirement through to the final erasure of the program from the system. The lifecycle may cover a number of years for even apparently trivial 'throw-away' programs, and in the commercial and military spheres it is likely to be measured in decades. Different authors have itemised a number of versions of the lifecycle; these versions only differ principally in the subdivisions of the main stages, which are generally accepted to be as follows.

(1)   Requirement identification (specification)
(2)   Program design
(3)   Coding
(4)   Module and program testing
(5)   Program maintenance

Various estimates based on the study of a number of large software-based systems suggest that, in the long term, the cost of the first four stages is likely to be only about one quarter of the cost of the fifth stage. The third stage of coding, which usually exerts a dominant influence upon our thinking, is now increasingly seen as a relatively minor part of the whole cycle of producing well-engineered software.

Of course these stages can be further subdivided; for example we can split the fourth stage into **module testing** and **integration testing**. Module testing is concerned with testing the functions of each module in isolation, while integration testing is more concerned with the behaviour of the whole program as each module is added in turn. The term **module** simply refers to a well-defined entity of code. For a concurrent system a module might be a complete process, while for a large sequential program it might be a procedure or function. In each case it is a well-identified and usually single-functioned whole.

Requirements is a large subject that is not really influenced by UNIX and the rest of this chapter is therefore concerned with stages 2 to 5 of the software lifecycle. We shall look at each of these and consider how the techniques described can be most effectively provided and supported with UNIX. However, this chapter is not concerned only with large software projects and large teams of programmers. The techniques discussed are applicable to all programs, however temporary (although many programs that begin as 'throw-away' code go on being used for years!). Equally, the benefits of a well-structured method of program production are as valuable to the single worker as to the project manager. Larger projects will obviously differ somewhat in the degree of emphasis that they need to give to some stages, but this is a reflection of greater financial motivation rather than necessarily greater need!

9.2   Designing programs

Programs do not grow; they need to be designed in some way. We cannot begin to design a program until we have at least some ideas about the problems that the program is to be used to solve—this is the problem of **specification**. Ideally the problem should be fully described and itemised before we begin designing our program, but it is in the nature of the real world that this cannot always be so, especially for scientific research where a part of the task is to identify the problem itself. In many cases, therefore, the program might also be regarded as being a prototype; i.e. the final version may need to be evolved on the basis of experience, using different versions of the program.

Even where the full specification cannot be produced, we must still begin with some objectives in mind, and these will form the basis of our design for the program. Even relatively trivial programs should be designed with some care, for the consequences of our design decisions can have very significant effects on the later stages of the software lifecycle. A well-designed program is easy to test and to modify, one that is badly designed can vastly increase the effort needed, as well as reducing the reliability of the finished product.

Various methods have been proposed for use in producing reliable and well-structured programs. Section 9.2.1 gives an introduction to one that has been quite widely adopted in various forms, and explains the procedures involved in producing a design by this method.

9.2.1   Top-down design

This approach is sometimes known by such labels as 'divide and conquer' or **stepwise refinement**. The object is gradually to break down the original large problem that we are attempting to use our program to solve into a set of smaller functional tasks, which can then be individually programmed and tested in a thorough and methodical fashion.

A good starting point is to write out a brief summary of the complete problem, e.g.

'convert all of the lower-case letters in a file of text into upper-case letters'

We can then examine the problem and try to identify the sub-tasks that are involved. For this particular example, we can identify three of these as follows:

  (i)   read a line of characters;
  (ii)   scan the line and modify any lower-case characters;
  (iii) write the modified line out again.

We can then continue this process of subdividing each of the new tasks into further levels of sub-tasks until it is felt that the sub-tasks identified cannot be usefully reduced any further; i.e. each one identified is doing one job. At this point in the process it is necessary to examine the various modules identified for the sub-tasks, to see if there is any redundancy among them. Certain quite distinct parts of the program may have common requirements from the low-level service routines—or, at least, requirements that can easily be adjusted to use some shared routines—and it would be inefficient to waste time in coding several versions of the same module.

Figure 9.5 shows the tree structure that typically emerges from this method for the simple example given above. In this case, as the problem is so very simple the resultant

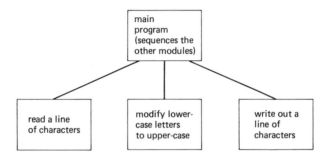

Fig. 9.5 Structure of a program to convert lower-case letters to upper-case

structure is not very pronounced, and there is no sharing of the lower-level modules. One feature of this method that may be evident is that most problems can easily lead us to producing a number of functionally equivalent but structurally different designs. This creative issue of the design process is beyond this simple introduction to the method, although some of the later sections will suggest some criteria that can be used to help the designer choose between the different possible designs. The reader who wishes to pursue the use of the top-down technique in more depth should refer to the references listed at the end of this chapter.

Various diagrammatic methods have been developed to help in the process of evolving, expressing and comparing software designs. Two particularly useful categories of these can be used to express the structure of the program from two very different viewpoints.

The hierarchical structure of the subprograms within a process can be shown by the use of a **structure chart**, a device originally proposed by L L Constantine. This shows the relationships between the various subprograms (i.e. which calls which), and indicates how data flows between them. It is particularly useful when assessing a design in terms of the degree of interdependence between the various subprograms, a factor which can significantly affect the ease with which changes can later be made to the design. Figure 9.6 shows a structure chart for the program that was described in Fig. 9.5, and the similarity of the structure is very evident, although the structure chart is a much more formal description. (There are no universally accepted conventions for drawing structure charts, although the conventions used do not vary widely.)

The second viewpoint is concerned with the flow of data through a program, and the structure of the program is described in terms of the sequences of actions that are performed upon the data. The **data flow diagram** is one means of expressing this

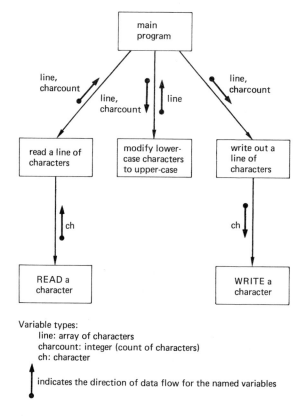

Fig. 9.6   A structure chart for the program to convert lower-case characters to upper-case

sequence, and Fig. 9.7 shows an example of such a diagram for the same problem as before. A rather more formal version of such a diagram has been adopted by the MASCOT scheme (Modular Approach to Software Construction, Operation and Test), to describe large software-based systems that are usually made up from a number of concurrent processes. The diagram is made up from four basic elements; Activities (processes), Channels ('pipelines'), Pools (shared databases) and devices. UNIX has facilities for producing programs which use parallel processes as components, so the resulting ACP diagram (Activity, Channel, Pool) can be an effective way of describing and designing these. Figure 9.8 shows a simple example of such a diagram.

Both the hierarchical and the data flow diagram techniques are useful to the programmer/designer when analysing a design, since they allow different aspects of the design to be assessed relatively easily. Note that the flow-chart has not been mentioned with these methods, although it is so widely known. The flow-chart is now regarded in

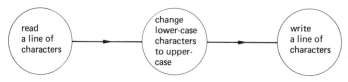

Fig. 9.7   A data flow diagram for the program to convert lower-case characters to upper-case

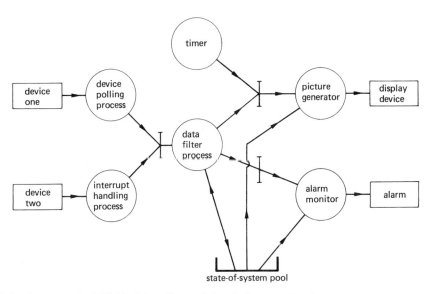

Fig. 9.8   An example ACP (Activity, Channel, Pool) diagram. The system illustrated is one which inputs data from two different devices: the first of these is polled on a regular basis, while the second is interrupt driven. The data read from these is analysed by a filter process, which updates the state-of-system pool and sends information to a picture generating process which displays the state of the system for an operator. An alarm process is called too, and this monitors the system to check that no critical situation has arisen; an alarm is sounded if one is detected

many circles as being too cumbersome to be of real use in expressing a design with any clarity—and is viewed by some authorities as being positively harmful in that it tends to encourage poor programming practices and structures. With the flow-chart the emphasis is placed very much upon the flow of control in terms of the detailed sequence of actions performed, whereas with more modern methods, the emphasis lies on the whole structure of the program, and so we are more readily able to assess how easily the program may be changed or updated in the future if a given structure is used. Sequencing information is also much better expressed as **Structured English** (pseudocode) and in this form is far more intelligible than the equivalent flow-chart for all but the most trivial problems.

9.2.2   Designing a conventional program

While a small number of problems can only be effectively solved by writing programs that use concurrency (i.e. simultaneous execution of more than one process), most of the problems that we deal with consist of applying a sequence of actions to the data that is read in, and are therefore well suited to conventional programming methods, and hence to the top-down design method.

Like any operating system, UNIX provides us with the means to produce programs to effect our designs in C, FORTRAN, Pascal or whichever other language is chosen as being the most suitable. On the whole the UNIX system does not particularly affect the choices that are made as a part of the process of design, except perhaps in such matters as input and output where the UNIX designer can conveniently use the standard input and standard output wherever possible, secure in the knowledge that these can be redirected as necessary.

For larger programs, the limitations on the address-space of the PDP-11 can become a problem, especially if the program needs to use large arrays or record structures that must be stored in memory. The virtual memory scheme of the larger PDP-11 models does provide some help by providing two sets of mapping registers, one set being used whenever the processor accesses instructions, and the other set being used whenever it accesses data. By using the '-i' option with the link-editor, *ld*, we can direct it to map the process so that it can use this facility and so effectively double the address range of the PDP-11: provided that our program does not need more than 32K words of memory for either the code or the data. The program is then referred to as using the **i and d space** facility.

On machines with a larger address space, such as the VAX-11 or the Motorola MC68000, this problem disappears, and the possible need to restrict data buffer sizes generally ceases to be a particular concern for the programmer.

9.2.3   Designing around the UNIX features

Section 9.2.1 outlined conventional program design as it can be performed for any operating system. This section is intended to suggest a few ways in which the particular strengths of UNIX can be utilised by the designer, together with some reasons for using them.

Many of the problems that are well suited to being solved using a computer involve having a solution where the program reads in some data and then processes or analyses it using a well-defined sequence of actions. A utility program such as *grep* is a good example of this; it reads a line of data (characters), passes this to its pattern matching routine, and if successful this then in turn passes the line of data to the output routine. Similarly a compiler is usually organised as a sequence of passes, with each pass in turn performing a further step in the analysis of the original program and towards the generation of its equivalent in executable machine language. Again, the data (in this case our source program) passes through a series of well-defined sub-tasks, being suitably reduced or modified on the way.

The data flow diagram is especially useful in helping us to express this type of design, and Fig. 9.9 shows such an example of processing, based upon a simple two-pass assembler.

The first pass reads through the source file, sizing the amount of storage needed to hold each instruction and creating a symbol table from the labels and their values. The second pass again reads the source file, and replaces symbolic references using labels with actual values so that it can perform the actual translation into the machine language. Figure 9.10 shows the same example, constructed in a conventional program form and expressed as a structure chart.

For a problem such as this, there is very little coupling between the two parts (i.e. the two passes). The only information that is shared, apart from the name of the input file, is the symbol table which is created by the first pass and used by the second pass. So the processing is highly sequential: the table is first created and then used—at no time is it being accessed from both parts of the program at once. This suggests that we can make each pass into a separate UNIX process and execute each in turn, passing the symbol table between them via a **pipe**, or in a temporary file. As we will see in a moment, the

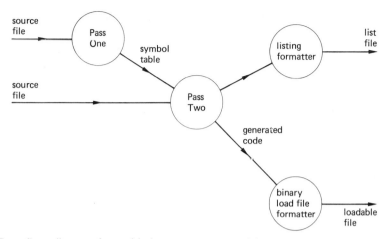

Fig. 9.9 Data flow diagram for a simple two-pass assembler

pipe also provides for the automatic sequencing of the processes and so is likely to be the more convenient solution, except where the symbol table may be so large that both parts of the program must handle it via a file rather than by just copying it into memory.

In this particular example there may be little to gain in splitting the program into two in this way, since neither part is likely to be re-usable for another assembler, and so a conventional program with two large subprograms for the passes may well be equally suitable as a design. For more complicated cases, though, the benefits of the second approach may be much greater. The individual parts may be too large for the whole program to be fitted into the available memory address space, or some of the parts may be re-usable for other programs—and writing them as separate programs will greatly

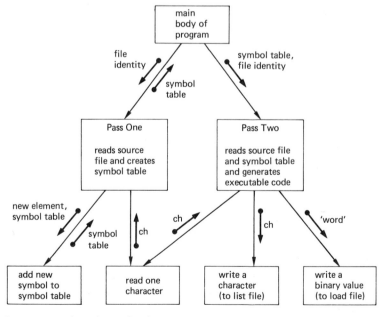

Fig. 9.10 A structure chart for a simple two-pass assembler

help with this. Before going on though to examine the benefits and disadvantages of constructing programs in this way, it is necessary to make a brief digression into the topic of pipes on UNIX in order to see more fully how they can be used for this approach.

Programming with the UNIX pipe

The pipe is a natural extension from the ideas of redirecting standard output and standard input for processes. Consider a program that is made up from three stages of processing, with the output from one stage being the input to the next. If each stage were written as a separate program, reading its data from the standard input and writing out the results of its processing on to the standard output, then we could write a shell program to perform the whole data processing sequence in the form:

```
pass1   <$1  >temp1
pass2   <temp1  >temp2
pass3   <temp2  >$2   ;   rm temp1 temp2
```

The first stage (program pass1) takes its input from the file that is specified as the first parameter of the shell program, and sends its output to the temporary file 'temp1'. The second stage takes its input from 'temp1' and writes in turn to the file 'temp2'. Then the third stage reads from 'temp2' and writes out the final processed data to the file specified as the second parameter of the shell program. Finally the files 'temp1' and 'temp2' are deleted.

One obvious potential problem is that the names 'temp1' or 'temp2' might already be in use, and while this can be fairly easily overcome, the general form of this sequence is so useful that UNIX provides an automatic mechanism for linking the standard output of one process to the standard input of another, namely the **pipe**. This takes the form of a temporary file that will automatically be deleted once used, and is denoted by the symbol

|

Our example shell program used above can now be rewritten, using pipes, as:

```
pass1 <$1 |   pass2   |   pass3 >$2
```

(Note that the '|' has the same effect on the *shell* as the ';', in allowing multiple shell program statements on a single line.)

A pipe is unidirectional (data flows only in one direction and there is no hand-shaking synchronisation involved within it), and no housekeeping of the temporary files is required from the programmer.

Some of the UNIX utility programs can be very useful when coupled to one's own programs by pipes. A program such as *grep* can be used to filter the input lines to a program, while *sort* can be used to re-order them (and of course they can be combined via a pipe to do both). Another utility which comes into its own in this way is *pr*, which is used to produce nicely formatted output, appropriately paginated and headed, and in multiple columns too, if required.

We can use pipes at any time, not just within shell programs, but it is in shell programming that they really come into their own. If the sub-tasks of our original problems are only loosely coupled, i.e. they do not depend upon sharing blocks of common data, then they can be made into programs rather than subprograms and joined together in sequence by pipes and shell program statements. While not every program can lend itself to this form of implementation, quite a large number can potentially be designed in this way and so it is worth examining some of the benefits that can be obtained from using this approach to program design and construction. These include the following:

(i) we can utilise existing modules (such as *sort*), rather than having to write our own;
(ii) because the individual programs are highly decoupled, it is possible to test the functions of each one in a clear and well-defined manner;
(iii) because each process has its own address space, some of the limitations of the PDP-11 address space restrictions can be avoided;
(iv) a program can be developed and tested on a step-by-step basis;
(v) we are not tied to one source language—each process can be formed using a program written in the most appropriate or convenient language.

The first two points are very much taken from the software engineering ethos, and both are highly desirable practices that such an approach encourages us to adopt. The existing modules need not only be UNIX utility programs; they can also be our own programs that have been used elsewhere. The point about testing is also very significant, since program testing (or debugging, though strictly this is a consequence of testing), can involve large amounts of time and effort—and the poorer the design, the greater the effort that is usually expended on this stage of development. So a good design practice can provide dividends for this stage.

The third point only affects very large programs, or programs that need large buffer spaces in memory. The major benefit is that we thus escape needing to organise memory overlay trees for the link-editor, with all of the problems that this usually involves.

Stepwise development of a program is a very big asset. Shell programming is particularly well suited to stepwise development, i.e. adding one new action at a time, and since the *shell* is interpretive, we also avoid the overheads of time required for frequent recompilation. The *echo* utility is useful too in allowing us to display the current values of the program variables at each stage of development.

Finally, mixing of source languages is also possible when constructing a conventional program. We can call routines that were written in C from programs that have been written in FORTRAN, for example, but it is a messy exercise to perform and needs some familiarity with parameter-passing conventions and with the internal naming conventions within the compilers. Using pipes and the *shell*, we can extract the maximum benefits from the available source languages without being bothered about such points.

There are clearly some disadvantages to be expected from making use of pipes in this way. Constructing our programs in this form will add to the execution overheads, since more than one process will need to be scheduled in and out of memory, and more data will be copied in and out of the filestore than would usually be necessary for conventional solutions. In practice though these overheads are rarely sufficient to be noticeable, given the power of the current generation of processors, and the extra overhead should not be an unduly significant handicap—when offset against the ease and speed of program development this provides.

There is considerable scope when using this method for producing prototype programs for the more problematic parts of a program, to be replaced by the final design at a later stage. Prototyping can be very useful when the user's requirements need to be clarified, because modification involves changes only to the appropriate component program, rather than having consequences throughout the whole program as commonly happens where data coupling exists between the parts of a conventional program.

9.3   Program construction

Having produced a design for our program, the details of each module being described via suitable diagrams combined with the use of structured English (say), it is then time to write the source code and enter it into the filestore. The process of design should be largely independent of the language to be used, although some dependence may creep in, particularly for the more numerically oriented applications.

Sections 9.3.1 to 9.3.3 consider some points about program construction, and how it might be effectively performed with the available languages and facilities in order to realise a design as a usable program.

9.3.1   Independent compilation

A design technique such as top-down naturally allies itself to the idea of constructing a program from a set of subprograms (which may be termed subroutines, functions, procedures, etc., according to the syntax of the particular language used). Generally these subprograms will correspond to the various modules that were identified in the design process.

The facility for independent compilation of such subprograms is described in Chapter 6. The idea is that each subprogram may be compiled and tested in isolation from the main program, and then the whole program can be put together using the link-editor in order to form the final process. Used with languages such as C and FORTRAN this allows us to concentrate our efforts on one sub-problem at a time, and used well it can considerably speed up the processes of debugging and testing of the code, since the functions of a subprogram should be sufficiently well-defined to allow systematic testing.

As an example of this last point, suppose that we have a subprogram whose function can be summarised as follows:

> 'determine whether or not the line of characters passed is a comment line, distinguished by the first character (other than tabs and spaces) being a semicolon'

To test this subprogram, we can simply input a number of lines where the result should be TRUE, i.e. it is a comment line. For example:

> a line with a semicolon in the first place;
> a line with spaces and tabs and a semicolon as the last character;
> a line with spaces and tabs preceding a semicolon, and further tabs and spaces plus other characters following it.

We should also input some samples of test data for which the result should be FALSE, such as:

> a line with no semicolon;
> a line with printing characters preceding a semicolon;
> a line with spaces, tabs and printing characters preceding a semicolon.

It is fairly easy to write a small main program which will input all of these cases in turn, possibly taking them from a test data file. By this method we can at least exercise this function in isolation, using most of the likely data forms that it will encounter.

The biggest disadvantage in using independent compilation in this manner is that the compiler only provides a limited degree of checking on the way in which the parts of the program fit together. At any one time it only has knowledge of the particular subprogram(s) that it is currently compiling and has no way of ensuring that references to other subprograms use the correct number or types of parameters when calling them. This can lead to mis-matches in the final program which the link-editor cannot detect either, and which can be tedious and difficult to isolate. As an example of this, consider a FORTRAN program which has been divided into two parts. In one file, 'main.f', we may have the main program body and a few subprograms, while in the file 'subs.f' we have the rest of the subprograms that are needed to create the whole program. If in this second file, one of the subprograms is defined as:

```
SUBROUTINE SWAP(X,Y)
INTEGER X(20),Y(20)
```

this indicates that the subroutine 'swap' expects to be called with two parameters, each being an array of type 'integer'. Unfortunately, if in 'main.f' we have the line

```
CALL SWAP(ALPHA,IMAGE,ISIZE)
```

i.e. the subroutine is being called with three parameters (which may or may not be of type 'integer'), then the compiler will still accept this because at the time of compiling 'main.f' it has no information to suggest how many parameters SWAP actually has. (In fact the FORTRAN compiler would not even necessarily check this point if it did have the information—this is one of the less secure FORTRAN features.) Another likely source of similar mis-matches is a COMMON block.

For a small program this is not too difficult to check by hand, but for larger programs, and programs that the programmer has not used for some time, it can be a serious problem. Indeed it was partly to show how such problems can be overcome that the Pascal language was designed in such a way that the whole program has to be submitted for compilation each time, so that the compiler can check for correctness of subprogram calls. (The later language Modula-2 has provided a more practical solution for larger programs, where Pascal requires the use of inconveniently large program files.) For languages such as C and FORTRAN which use independent compilation, there is not much that can be done about subprogram calls, since the compilers themselves are not designed to perform any checking. One thing that can be done though is to ensure that global data, as exemplified by the COMMON blocks of FORTRAN, is supplied via the use of an 'include' file. Chapter 6 gave an example of how this can be done, and it is a good practice to adopt the habit of building up such '.h' files when constructing programs in these languages. Even the use of the 'include' cannot be a complete guarantee of data integrity, since any change to the '.h' file requires that all the files using it should be recompiled. One way to do this is to name one's files judiciously so as to allow the metacharacter pair [. . .] to be used as in the following form:

```
$ f77 myprog[1-6].f
```

Here the complete program is made up from the files 'myprog1.f' to 'myprog6.f' and the whole program can thus be recompiled at once to ensure that any changes are incorporated throughout. (We will later be looking at examples of the use of the utility *make*, which often solves this particular problem.)

Data can of course be split among a number of '.h' files, since we can use multiple 'include' statements. In this way we can logically group variable and constant definitions so as to aid in their maintenance by making them more easily located and identified. Since 'include' files can themselves use the 'include' statement, there is considerable flexibility available to meet any particular need we can devise.

9.3.2 Pre-processors

When introducing the *ratfor* version of FORTRAN in Chapter 6, it was described there as being implemented via a **pre-processor** program. Pre-processors are an example of using the design structure discussed earlier, with a sequence of processors passing the data along a chain. The **macro** facility common in many assemblers is another example of pre-processing. One advantage of pre-processors is that they can provide some common interfaces and definitions for use by a team of programmers whose modules are eventually to be fitted together.

A pre-processor program simply manipulates strings of characters, or 'text'. Taking a set of initial definitions, e.g.

    LENGTH = 64

it scans the given input file to see if it can find any matches to the defined strings, in this case the string 'LENGTH'. Whenever a match is found, the characters of the string are replaced by the new characters provided in the original definition, in this case the characters '6' and '4'.

What usually makes the pre-processor particularly useful is the ability to handle definitions that have parameters within them, and to make the appropriate substitutions for them when the function is used. Unlike a subprogram, the use of pre-processing generates no special calling codes in the final executable program image file; all that happens is that text substitution occurs before the actual file is compiled or assembled.

UNIX provides us with the general purpose pre-processor (or 'macro expansion') program *m4*. *m4* can be used to pre-process a source file before it is submitted to the appropriate compiler, and as with *ratfor*, this might allow the use of constructs that are not normally a part of the standard language. Another use is the grouping together of frequently repeated sequences of actions. So the earlier point about the UNIX assembler *as* lacking macro facilities is really a little unfair, since these can be provided by the separate program *m4* in accordance with the UNIX tradition of one task—one program. The pipe is of course a natural adjoint to the use of *m4*, to couple it together with the final compiler.

The biggest problem of a practical nature that arises from the use of a pre-processor is that any error messages from the compiler that are prefixed with a line number may be rather hard to match to the source listing of the program, since these refer to the text-processed file that was submitted to the compiler rather than to the file that the programmer is using.

9.3.3 Other program development aids

The features mentioned so far have been concerned with trying to improve upon the limitations of existing languages, or with trying to aid program development as performed by a group of programmers. Two other UNIX features that can aid with the organisation of program development are subdirectories and library files. Used with a little planning, these can both make the housekeeping of one's files, as well as the actual coding of programs, much easier to manage.

The use of subdirectories needs a little forethought. Most programs will start off as one or two files of source code, however large they are finally destined to be, and the number of files used will usually increase either by plan or by natural evolution of the program. Subdirectories can be used to group files that make up distinct parts of the program, and which can possibly be developed and tested as an isolated group. This is particularly true of the style of program design described in Section 9.2.3, using a sequence of separate processes—and particularly where the group of files make up a program unit that might well be used elsewhere too. In particular, any 'include' files can be grouped into a subdirectory, probably called 'h'!

An associated issue is that of documentation produced with a program, and which can be gathered together in another subdirectory. Figure 9.11 shows a possible directory tree for use with the development of a program which is to be made up from three sequential processes, linked together by pipes.

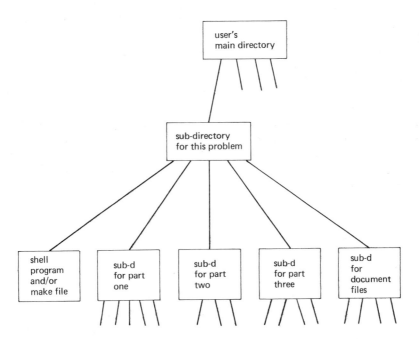

Fig. 9.11 A subdirectory tree structure for managing the construction of a three-part program. Each of the three main subdirectories will contain source and binary files. There may be another subdirectory for any '.h' files that are shared

The more experienced UNIX user is usually marked by generous use of the subdirectory facility, and it is well worth developing the habit of using subdirectories to partition up a problem as part of a general development philosophy based on an engineering approach to software development.

The other useful method for grouping files is to use the library structure as created by the utility *ar*. Libraries are usually used as a means of grouping a number of related object files together, so that the link-editor can select those that are required for a particular application without any user involvement. Contrary to much popular belief, libraries are quite easy to create and maintain—and while they are not necessarily as generally useful a feature as subdirectories, their use on appropriate occasions is highly recommended.

9.4   Testing programs on UNIX

All but the most trivial of programs need to be tested in some way, either during their development or when complete. By **testing**, we usually mean that the program is checked in some way to see whether or not it performs the sequence of actions originally specified. (Some checking will be done by the compiler, which will check that the actions specified within a program are to some degree self-consistent, but of course this cannot check the actions against the original specification in any way.)

Any form of testing will usually require the use of some form of **test data**, i.e. a set of inputs which have been selected to exercise the appropriate parts of the program, and for which we can predict the expected results—which may then be compared with the results actually obtained. Unfortunately, as a program becomes larger and more complex, it becomes much harder to test it exhaustively or systematically without the use of very large amounts of test data. Even small programs can have many complex combinations of conditions to be tested, and so complete testing of every facet can rapidly become an exorbitant overhead. Sections 9.4.1 to 9.4.3 are concerned with examining one way in which the testing can be methodically performed on a step-by-step basis, much as we evolved the original design.

9.4.1   Development and testing using stubs and drivers

Designing a program by using a top-down technique will usually result in the form of structure shown in Fig. 9.6. The main body of such a program will be concerned with providing data storage for some key variables, and with sequencing the calls to the subprograms to perform their specific tasks.

If we have managed to produce a design in which the sub-tasks (i.e. the subprograms) are highly functional, each dealing with only one particular job, and having minimal dependence upon the actions of any other sub-tasks at the same level of the hierarchy (i.e. no global or shared variables), then it will usually be practical to code and test each subprogram in turn. While this method will not exhaustively exercise all possible routes through a program, it does permit us at least to test each sub-task thoroughly, and so forms a good approximation to the effect that we are seeking. This is effectively module testing followed by integration testing.

The **stubs and drivers** technique is a method for doing just this, and although on first acquaintance it may seem to involve much more work than the traditional method of 'coding up the lot and stirring it around', in practice the development time needed for a program will almost always be reduced by its use. Essentially it involves developing and testing the code in a stepwise manner, much as the original design was originally reached by progressive refinement.

To use the method the following conditions should be satisfied:

(i)   an acceptance by the programmer of the fact that programs do not work correctly the first time they are keyed in;

(ii)   a reasonably well-structured design so that the sub-tasks are well-defined and single-functioned;

(iii) little or no use of global variables to communicate between the subprograms (i.e. data is all passed as parameters of the subprogram call).

The last requirement reiterates the engineering assumption that saving processor time is no longer the sole criteria of a 'good program', and that data should always be passed in and out of subprograms via parameters to allow a more structured control and checking to be performed.

The stubs and drivers method is implemented by using the following recipe.

(1) First create the program by entering the code for the main body and dummy subprograms (the 'stubs' and 'drivers').
(2) Pass this version through the compiler until it compiles correctly (i.e. allowing us to catch and correct minor keying errors and coding slips).
(3) Now replace one of the dummy subprograms with its actual code.
(4) Pass the new version of the program through the compiler, correcting any keying errors as necessary.
(5) Use an appropriate set of test data values to test the functions of the subprogram just added (i.e. module testing).
(6) Use another set of test data to test the actions of the whole program up to this point (i.e. integration testing).
(7) Repeat steps 3 to 6 until the whole program is complete.

The advantage of using this method is that it follows the programmer's golden rule, which is to change only one thing at a time. By doing so we can concentrate our efforts on testing the actions of one new function (step 5) and so can select our test data on a well-defined basis. It should also be more obvious now why the use of global variables is considered to be undesirable, since their use may make it necessary to check back on earlier modules when expanding later modules that share data with them. This weakens the modularity and makes step 6 even more complex than it already will be!

So far we have neglected to clarify the difference between a 'stub' and a 'driver'. Both are a form of dummy subprogram, but whereas a stub simply takes data in, i.e. acts as a data **sink**, a driver will also generate an output of some form, (e.g. a FORTRAN function subprogram would need to have a dummy driver in order to be able to return a value). To make this clearer, Figs 9.12 to 9.14 show the development by this method of the simple program example that was developed in Section 9.2 to change lower-case letters in its input to upper-case letters. This solution uses one stub (the routine to output the completed line), and two drivers (the routine to read a line and the routine to modify the characters of a line: the latter could possibly have also been a stub, depending on the order of expansion preferred).

9.4.2 Using stubs and drivers on UNIX

The methodology described in Section 9.4.1 is a general one that can be used for developing programs on any operating system. However, UNIX provides some features that make it particularly suitable for the use of this form of development. The most obvious facility to use is the redirection of standard input and standard output. This can be used to make the entering of test data something that can be done manually or from a previously prepared data file, and can be used to allow the outputs to be easily routed off to a file for later analysis. Reading through the results of a test run is definitely a desk

```
(*  An example of program development via the methods of stubs
    and drivers, for a program to convert any lower-case letters
    in its output to upper-case letters.
*)

PROGRAM convert(INPUT,OUTPUT);
CONST
    maxline = 79;                 (* assume maximum line of 80 chars *)
TYPE
    buffer = ARRAY [0..maxline] OF CHAR· (* line buffer type *)
VAR
    line : buffer;                (* buffer to hold current line *)
    charcount : INTEGER·          (* line size buffer *)

(*  dummy version of procedure to read a line of text *)

PROCEDURE readaline(VAR newline : buffer; VAR length · INTEGER);
BEGIN
    newline[0] := 'a';  newline[1] := 'B'; (* some test data *)
    newline[2] := 'y';  newline[3] := 'Z';
    length := 4;
END; (* readaline *)

(*  procedure to write a converted line out again *)

PROCEDURE writealine(newform : buffer; length : INTEGER);
VAR
    index : INTEGER;
BEGIN
    FOR index := 0 TO (length-1) DO BEGIN
        WRITE(newform[index])    END;
    WRITELN·                     (* flush output buffers *)
END; (* writealine *)

(*  dummy version of procedure to do the conversion *)

PROCEDURE change(VAR nextline : buffer; length · INTEGER);
BEGIN
    (* no action at all *)
END; (* change *)

(*  *** main body of program     *** *)

BEGIN
    WHILE NOT EOF DO BEGIN
        readaline(line,charcount);
        change(line,charcount);
        writealine(line,charcount);
    END;     (* while loop *)
END. (* convert *)
```

Fig. 9.12 Development by stubs and drivers—first version

```
(*  An example of program development via the methods of stubs
    and drivers, for a program to convert any lower-case letters
    in its output to upper-case letters.
*)

(*  second version - procedure readaline expanded *)
PROGRAM convert(INPUT,OUTPUT);
CONST
    maxline = 79;                (* assume maximum line of 80 chars *)
TYPE
    buffer = ARRAY [0..maxline] OF CHAR; (* line buffer type *)
VAR
    line : buffer;              (* buffer to hold current line *)
    charcount : INTEGER;           (* line size buffer *)

(*  procedure to read a line of text *)
PROCEDURE readaline(VAR newline : buffer; VAR length : INTEGER);
BEGIN
    length := 0;
    WHILE NOT EOLN AND NOT EOF DO BEGIN
        READ(newline[length]);
        length := length + 1;
    END;    (* while *)
    READLN;      (* flush buffer *)
END; (* readaline *)

(*  procedure to write a converted line out again *)
PROCEDURE writealine(newform : buffer; length : INTEGER);
VAR
    index : INTEGER;
BEGIN
    FOR index := 0 TO (length-1) DO BEGIN
        WRITE(newform[index])    END;
    WRITELN;                 (* flush output buffers *)
END; (* writealine *)

(*  dummy version of procedure to do the conversion *)
PROCEDURE change(VAR nextline : buffer; length : INTEGER);
BEGIN
    (* no action at all *)
END; (* change *)

(*  *** main body of program    *** *)

BEGIN
    WHILE NOT EOF DO BEGIN
        readaline(line,charcount);
        change(line,charcount);
        writealine(line,charcount);
    END;    (* while loop *)
END. (* convert *)
```

Fig. 9.13 Stubs and drivers example—second version

```
(*  An example of program development via the methods of stubs
    and drivers, for a program to convert any lower-case letters
    in its output to upper-case letters.
*)

(*  third version - procedure change expanded *)

PROGRAM convert(INPUT,OUTPUT);
CONST
    maxline = 79·               (* assume maximum line of 80 chars *)
TYPE
    buffer = ARRAY [0..maxline] OF CHAR; (* line buffer type *)
VAR
    line : buffer;              (* buffer to hold current line *)
    charcount : INTEGER;          (* line size buffer *)

(*  procedure to read a line of text *)

PROCEDURE readaline(VAR newline : buffer; VAR length : INTEGER);
BEGIN
    length := 0;
    WHILE NOT EOLN AND NOT EOF DO BEGIN
        READ(newline[length]);
        length := length + 1·
    END;    (* while *)
    READLN;      (* flush buffer *)
END; (* readaline *)

(*  procedure to write a converted line out again *)

PROCEDURE writealine(newform : buffer; length : INTEGER);
VAR
    index : INTEGER;
BEGIN
    FOR index := 0 TO (length-1) DO BEGIN
        WRITE(newform[index])    END;
    WRITELN;                  (* flush output buffers *)
END; (* writealine *)

(*  procedure to convert lower-case letters to the upper-case
    letter.  Uses basis of ASCII coding that difference is that
    lower-case letter has bit 5 of the code set, so clear this
    to convert to the upper-case character. *)

PROCEDURE change(VAR nextline : buffer; length : INTEGER);
VAR
    index : INTEGER;
BEGIN
    FOR index := 0 TO (length-1) DO BEGIN
        IF nextline[index] IN ['a'..'z'] THEN
        nextline[index] := CHR( ORD(nextline[index]) - 32 );
    END; (* for *)
END; (* change *)                              (*continued*)
```

```
(*  *** main body of program   *** *)

BEGIN
    WHILE NOT EOF DO BEGIN
        readaline(line,charcount);
        change(line,charcount);
        writealine(line,charcount);
    END;    (* while loop *)
END. (* convert *)
```

Fig. 9.14 Stubs and drivers example—third and final version

job, and not one for the terminal session; this facility makes it much easier to support this approach.

Another aid is the pipe. Using this the output of the program can be run through a filter (say *grep* or a similar facility), to select those cases that we are currently interested in, and so aiding our analysis by reducing the scope for human error. A utility such as *sort* can also help with this by re-ordering the output, and so helping us to be able to analyse it using a form that is suited to the problem and to our analysis.

This method for program development is also suited to programs that are made up from a series of UNIX processes, connected by pipes. The stub might then be a process which ignores its inputs, or just passes them on, while the driver is a process that generates test data. Shell programs can similarly be developed in this manner too, since the organisation of calling a process from a process is much the same as that of calling subprograms from a program.

9.4.3 The use of backup files

The UNIX philosophy of only keeping one copy (version) of a file was introduced very early in Part I. While in general this proves to be no real inconvenience, there are occasions when we may prefer to keep the previous version of a file that has just been modified—perhaps to protect against accidental erasure, or as a means of checking that the correct changes were applied (the utility *diff* comes in useful for that task). This is also something that is useful when developing via a stubs and drivers method, where we may need to check that a particular change has been made correctly in expanding one of the modules, or may even decide that the order of expansion is proving wrong and wish to move back a step. On UNIX as it stands, this does not prove to be a very simple exercise.

The shell program given below provides a new form for using the *ed* text editor via the program 'eb' (of course it can be stored in a file of any name, and for that matter could invoke any other text editor besides *ed*). It is fairly simple and the effects can be rather easily circumnavigated by using the 'w' command within *ed* with a new filename as its argument, but it does provide a simple backup facility and demonstrates the ease with which such tools can be created using the shell programming facilities. In this form the backup file is given a name which is generated by appending '_b' to the name of the original file—so restricting this to twelve letters or characters. The form of the program in structured English is as follows:

```
IF there is one parameter to the process call
THEN
      IF the file passed as a parameter already exists
      THEN
            make up a temporary filename using the process
                number
            copy the current version of the file to the
                temporary filename
            edit the current version of the file
            move the temporary version of the file to the backup
                file (overwriting any existing backup file)
      ELSE
            just edit and create a new file
      ENDIF
ELSE
      write a message to indicate an incorrect number of
          parameters
ENDIF
```

(This reiterates the use of normal top-down methods to design shell programs too.)
The actual shell program can then be written very concisely in the form:

```
: This shell program provides an edit_backup facility
: with the backup file having the same name as the
: original file with '_b' appended to it
:
if test $# -eq 1
then
     if test -s $1
     then
          tempname=$$temp
          cp $1 $tempname
          ed $1
          mv $tempname $1_b
     else
          ed $1
     fi
else
     echo "filename missing or too many names"
fi
```

There are a few points to notice about this particular example, both in terms of shell programming facilities and also in terms of the manner in which such a program can be implemented. These are as follows.

(1)   Comments can be included in shell programs by preceding them with the character ':', followed by a space or a tab character before the first printing character.

(2)   The temporary filename has been created using '$$'; this obtains the (unique) process number, which is then used as part of the string making up a unique filename.

(3) The *shell* is fussy about some syntax points, especially the need for space or tab characters after a ':'; and also in requiring no spaces around the '=' symbol, as when assigning 'tempname'.

This scheme only gives a backup copy of a source (text) file, but since binary files can be easily regenerated by compiling the source files, this is usually more than sufficient and is far less wasteful of filestore than a system that insists on maintaining every version of any form of file.

9.5 Maintenance of software

As explained in Section 9.1, maintenance can include the modification of our own programs as well as the conversion or modification of programs which have been written by others, and which may have been run under other operating systems. An example of the latter class of program is the cross-assembler. Cross-assembler programs for many microprocessors have been written in a standard language such as FORTRAN so that they are portable between different host operating systems. Inevitably some system-dependent features will be present, particularly where input and output conventions are involved, and so some modification will be required to adapt the program to run on another operating system. Another possible source of problems might be the use of different word sizes between host computers, with implications for any storage-dependent features; however this can be, and usually is, avoided in the program design.

Sections 9.5.1 and 9.5.2 look at some of the problems that are involved in maintaining programs, and describe some of the UNIX features that may be particularly useful in performing the tasks involved.

9.5.1 Maintaining your own programs

The ease with which a program can be modified will be very much influenced by the structure that it has, i.e. it will depend upon the original design. Indeed, one of the methods of assessing the quality of a design is to do just this: to consider what likely changes will be required of a program, and how easily a particular design can be adapted. In a good design, most likely changes should only affect a few (ideally only one) of the program modules that were identified in the top-down decomposition. From this point of view, the use of global variables shared between subprograms will usually weaken their independence and can complicate the task of modification considerably.

Unfortunately the nature of many scientific and engineering applications makes it quite difficult to determine whether a given program will have a long life, and whether it will undergo any substantial changes in this period. Ideally, this can be overcome by ensuring that all programs are systematically designed and thoroughly documented—but since most of us fall short of such an ideal we still require the support of a number of software tools to aid us in maintenance.

Designing for eventual changes
It is in the nature of scientific work that answers are frequently only known very imperfectly, if at all, at the start of an item of research or development. For such problems, we may not be able to specify very thoroughly what the program is eventually to do, and there are therefore very good arguments for trying to build it in such a way that it will be fairly easy to change. The key to this is **modular design**.

One of the problems of the top-down design method is that for some problems we may be able to identify a number of equivalent solutions, based on rather different choices of sub-tasks. From the viewpoint of functionality and effectiveness there may well be very little to differentiate between the designs produced. One means that can be used to assess them, and to select a preferred form, is to consider the likely forms of change that will occur to the program. (Note that it is the form of the change that matters, not the details of how it will change. As an example of this, the form might be a change to 'a new format of filename'. What matters is that the format might change, not what the new format will be in itself.) This form of analysis was proposed in 1972 by D L Parnas, as a part of a very influential paper, although the difficulty of formulating procedural rules for performing such an analysis has rather inhibited its adoption on a wide basis. However, even intuitive assessment of this type is better than none, and may be highly effective where we are dealing with familiar problems.

In terms of the very simple example used earlier, of a program to change lower-case letters in a file to upper-case letters, we might like to consider which modules would require modification if the following aspects of use were changed:

> the program were to be run on a machine using a different basis for character storage (e.g. EBCDIC instead of ASCII);
> the program were to be run on a machine using a different format within the file structure;
> other characters, outside the alphabetic set, were to need change; e.g. the ';' to a '/' say.

For each of these in turn, we could examine our design and list the modules (procedures) that would need to be modified. Obviously this not only reflects the design, but also to some extent the way in which we can code it—the greater the degree of logical abstraction that a language provides, the easier it is to avoid difficulties with detail. It may also therefore influence the way in which we program!

A useful forward look to take during program design is therefore to perform this form of analysis, even on an *ad hoc* basis, and to be prepared to make changes to our design where we find that some possible changes might require extensive or complex modifications. By aiming to confine changes to only a few modules we will reduce the time later needed to re-familiarise ourselves with the detailed workings of our program (this is always longer than expected). We will also make the task of testing the effects of changes much easier, since if we are only re-testing a few modules we can concentrate our attention upon them more effectively.

Reconstructing programs—the make *utility*

Where a program becomes very large, and is composed by compiling a number of different source and 'include' files, or where we have a number of closely associated programs where a change in one of them may require recompilation of the whole group, the organisation of program construction can become both tedious and difficult—and hence potentially unreliable. For this reason, the UNIX system includes a *make* utility program which utilises a command file structure as an aid to program construction. *make* is very simple to use, though less simple to set up, partly because of the power that it provides. It also possesses a considerable brevity of style within its command files, even by UNIX standards.

Since we can perform straightforward recompilation of any number of files simply by writing a shell program, the obvious question to be asked is what extra benefits are available from using *make*. The first one, which can be significant for large programs being constructed on a busy system, is that *make* looks to see which files involved have been modified since it last performed its task, and then recompiles only those that have been changed, together with any that are dependent upon them. As an example of this feature, if we have a program which is built up from, say, twelve source files, and these in turn use various combinations of three 'include' files, then a change to one of the 'include' files will result in the next *make* session recompiling only the files that depend upon that one file, and re-using any object files that were previously compiled for the others.

Obviously the use of *make* with simple programs is rather pointless, apart from for practice purposes (and *make* is the sort of program to encourage practice!). To be worthwhile the results have to be quite large and complex—as an example, most of the larger UNIX utilities are maintained in this way, e.g. the FORTRAN compiler. This brings in another feature of *make*, which is the selectivity that is possible. We can label the commands within the 'make' command file, and thereby selectively reconstruct all or part of our system by passing the appropriate label as a parameter of *make*. To return to the FORTRAN compiler, constructing this involves rebuilding the compiler itself, and also the associated library files, for which the sources must be compiled and the results archived via *ar*. A full 'make' will construct compiler and libraries afresh, but equally we can choose just to rebuild the compiler or a single library should our change only require this.

A single 'make' command file can therefore be used to maintain a program, and also any associated libraries and other programs, thus simplifying and centralising the task of maintenance. Much of the strength of *make* lies in this ability to aid the maintenance or construction of a whole package of software as required.

When used, *make* will by default look for its commands in a file called 'makefile', and these commands are a mix of *shell* commands and of information about the dependencies of one file upon another. Figure 9.15 shows an example of such a file. In this example, the program 'variance' is made up from the files 'main.f' and 'subs.f' (clearly FORTRAN source files), and these in turn use the 'include' file 'commons.h' to hold the details of

```
# a command file for the make program
# to construct program 'variance' from
# two separate files, main.f and subs.f
# N.B command lines are preceded by a 'tab' character

variance: main.o subs.o
    f77 main.o subs.o -o variance

main.o: commons.h main.f
    f77 -cu main.f

subs.o: commons.h subs.f
    f77 -cu subs.f
```

Fig. 9.15   An example 'makefile' for the make program

the COMMON blocks that they share. Note that comment lines can be used in the 'makefile', and begin with the character '#'.

The first line of instructions tells *make* that the item 'variance' depends upon the two files 'main.o' and 'subs.o' (the ':' character indicates dependence). This is then followed by the *shell* command used to create 'variance', calling *ld* via *f77*. The next two pairs of lines indicate how to construct 'main.o' and 'subs.o' in turn, and indicate their dependence on 'commons.h'. The compiler options to suppress the link-editor stage (–c) and to use the 'undefined' facility (–u) are also requested, as being good practice to adopt generally.

So typing the command

    $ make

will cause *make* to seek out 'makefile' and to execute the commands it finds in there. Note that if we have only changed (say) 'main.f' since the last construction session then *make* will recognise that 'subs.o' is still valid and only reconstruct 'main.o'. It also echoes the *shell* commands as they are executed—which keeps the user informed about exactly what is happening.

make is not a particularly simple program to use or to set up. Examining the various versions of 'makefile' in the system directories might help a little, but for first use the user is advised to let the 'makefile' grow with the development of the program, i.e. by extending it to include each new module as it is added, rather than trying to switch to using *make* when the program starts to get unwieldy.

9.5.2 Modifying another's programs

Programs that have been acquired from other systems can involve the programmer in a lot of work, simply to become familiar enough with their structure in order to be able to make any changes—which might include the changes necessary to make them run under UNIX. Additionally, such programs may well be large; the earlier example of a cross-assembler program is typical of such a program which can run into many thousands of lines of source code. Following the principles of stepwise refinement of our problems, we now consider some of the issues involved: those of handling large files on UNIX, and those of modifying a largely unknown program that has been written by another programmer.

Handling large files on UNIX
The biggest problem with handling large files is that the *ed* text editor has a limit on the maximum size of interactive buffer that it can support, and while this is large enough to hold, typically, several thousand lines of source code, sooner or later a program will be too large for this limit.

Since most UNIX utility programs such as compilers have no difficulty in taking their inputs from a sequence of files and concatenating them, and the *shell* metacharacters enable these to be very concisely expressed with the aid of a little judicious selection of file naming conventions, the obvious solution is to divide the over-large program into a sequence of smaller files. There is a *split* utility program which will do just this. The resultant files can then be conveniently handled by *ed* and recombined via the metacharacters on input to the translator.

split simply divides a file into a set of files of the given length, so inevitably this will result in some subprograms being divided across the bounds of two of the new files. This can easily be remedied with the aid of the *tail* utility, which extracts the last *n* lines of a file, together with the text editor 'r' command to copy one file to another. Should we need to recombine our files at any point, then of course this is one of the tasks that can be performed by *cat* (remember—con*cat*enate!).

As a short example of this, if we have a very large FORTRAN source program stored in the file 'analyser.f' then we can divide it up into (say) three files, by using the command

```
$ split -1200 analyser.f partanalys
```

The original file will be divided up into blocks of 1200 lines, and stored in the files 'partanalysa', 'partanalysb', and 'partanalysc'. The original file, 'analyser.f', is left unchanged.

If the original file were 3400 lines long, then the first two of these files would each be 1200 lines long, while the last will have a length of only 1000 lines. (If the file length is not specified in the command, *split* uses a default size of 1000 lines.)

Using *mv* we can then rename the files as 'analyser1.f', 'analyser2.f', and 'analyser3.f', and compile the whole program via the command

```
$ f77 analyser[1-3].f
```

Converting programs—a note about conventions

When transferring a program between any two operating systems, there are likely to be some changes needed, even for a standard language, since file handling is usually rather system specific. In addition, for languages such as FORTRAN, there may well be local extensions provided on the compiler, and these may have been used by the original programmer.

We can use the UNIX facilities to automate some of the changes that might be needed. As an example, a fairly common extension provided for the FORTRAN language is the ability to specify integer constants to base eight (octal), rather than to decimal. For the PDP-11 compilers produced by DEC, the convention chosen is that such a constant is specified by preceding the numeric characters by the character 'o' or 'O', as in

```
o102   or   O102
```

On the UNIX system the *f77* compiler also supports such an extension, but this requires that the constant should be preceded by such a letter, and that the numeric field should be in quotes, as in

```
o'102'   or   O'102'
```

The conversion between these is fairly easy with the *ed* text editor. (As a hint, look for the pattern specified by

```
o[1-7]
```

as a start point.) You may use the global change facility ('g'). It is prudent though to begin by making a copy of the original file!

More drastic differences might include the use of different character sets from the widely used ASCII codes described in this book. Two useful utility programs to help with changes of that type are the programs *tr* and *dd*. The latter includes the ability to interchange between widely used character sets as a standard set of options.

A program 'acquaint'
One of the problems of converting programs is that the documentation available for them is rarely complete in any way, and so the programmer may be faced with a large program and given relatively little idea of how it is structured or even works. While a line-numbered listing is obviously the first thing to be generated, and then studied, the *grep* utility can considerably aid an exploration into the structure of the program.

   grep enables us to build up various cross-reference lists. As an example of this, if we are examining the use and action of a sub-program called 'dumpblock' (say), then we can find all the parts of the program that refer to 'dumpblock' by searching for that string. This can be done using the command

```
$ grep -n dumpblock newprogram.p
```

(assuming that our program is stored in 'newprogram.p'). Using the '–n' option with *grep* will give us a print-out of each reference, including the line number, which is particularly useful in matching our information to our program listing. Working with *grep* in this way we can soon identify where and how particular procedures and variables are used within a program—using redirection of the standard output when necessary in order to keep copies of our output.

   When working on a large program, while *grep* soon becomes indispensable, it is also worth reducing the typing effort by creating a one-line shell program, such as the program 'scan' given below:

```
grep -n $1 newprogram.p
```

Our earlier search can be summarised more elegantly as

```
$ scan dumpblock
```

which is much easier to type. (*grep* is so addictive that one soon comes to wonder how you ever managed without it!)

9.6   Summary

This has been a very large chapter, dealing heavily with concepts, but it is central to the text since it deals with the ways in which a programmer can exploit the very features that make UNIX so different an operating system. It would be too ambitious to claim that the methods suggested are the only ways of tackling different problems, nor that they are always even the best way for a particular problem; but they are general enough and structured enough to form good practices for the UNIX programmer to adopt in making good use of what the UNIX system has to offer.

References

Software engineering is a large topic, and the literature rarely attempts to cover more than a few topics from the whole. The references below offer quite a good starting point for anyone wishing to follow up some of the points made in this chapter.

1. A good general introduction to the topic of Software Engineering, and a good source of references is:
   Software Engineering. Sommerville, I, Addison-Wesley, 1982.
2. A more specialist approach to design, from two of the 'gurus' of the subject, is:
   Structured Design. Constantine, L L and Yourdon, E, Prentice-Hall, 1979.
3. An influential paper on assessment of design, but fairly detailed in its arguments, is:
   'On the Criteria to be used in decomposing Systems into Modules'. Parnas, D L, *Comms ACM*, **15,** 1053–1058, 1972.

10
Text handling on UNIX—and the *roff* programs

10.1 Introduction

The user of an operating system such as the UNIX system is mainly concerned with handling two quite distinct forms of text. The first form consists of program source files, i.e. files that are made up from program statements and which can be used as input to the appropriate compiler. This form of text is sometimes just referred to as **code** (we ignore for the moment the fact that such code will normally include comment statements too). The layout and format of such files will be constrained to a varying degree by the particular requirements of the computer language being used, but the file is still just a file of characters as far as UNIX is concerned—it is the use that we make of it that distinguishes it in any way.

The second form of text is those files that make up **documents** (as opposed to the comment blocks used in programs). That is, the text now consists of natural language statements to be processed by the human eye rather than by the machine, although we may desire to constrain the format in some way still in order to make the use of the documents more convenient.

This chapter describes how both of these forms of file can be stored, accessed, modified, maintained and used on the UNIX system, and the facilities that are available for performing layout organisation for document files in particular.

10.2 Common features of text files

The division of text files into two classes as suggested above is in many ways one that requires some form of discrimination to be performed by the human user. As far as the processes that handle the use of filestore are concerned, any file is simply a string of characters, and a text file is really only distinguished from any other file in that the characters used are all taken from the subset of printable characters. Certainly there is nothing in such a file that would allow a program to make the distinction between the types of text file that was made above. So the aid of the human user is required to make this distinction in some way, usually by adopting conventions of extensions to filenames, and perhaps also by the choice of filenames themselves.

For many purposes our documentation files can be maintained and modified using the same set of software tools that are used to change source files, so emphasising the need to be able to distinguish between them by the use of naming conventions. Since program files usually have extensions such as

        .c , .f , .p   etc.

one quite adequate convention is to use numeric extensions such as

        .1 , .2 , .3   etc.

In practice, many programmers also find it useful to separate their source files and documentation files into separate subdirectories, usually at the same level of the directory hierarchy, and then to consider the maintenance of the two forms as being essentially one task.

Until now, our main concern has been with the use of files used as source programs, rather than with files that are to be used as reports or memoranda, etc. Yet from the beginning, the UNIX system was designed so that users would have powerful text processing facilities to support their programming, and so that these would be integrated with the general UNIX philosophy in such a way that the techniques described in Part I can also be used for handling documents too.

However, the text processing features of UNIX are just that; 'text' processing rather than 'word' processing. The text processing tools are meant to be compatible with the general programming tools and methods—and are therefore not especially geared for use by the non-programmer, although reports of use do suggest that this is not a particularly great hurdle to overcome. (This perhaps offers more scope for shell programming techniques.)

The ability to maintain code alongside the related documentation is a facility which can only be an aid to program development if used well, since it simplifies one area that has long been a particular problem of software engineering. It is a common experience that programmers much prefer writing code to writing any form of description of it—but at least on UNIX the two can be performed at the same time, using the same text editor, and the programmer is able to maintain the two side-by-side and without having to use hand-patched documents either.

Too much change can be a bad thing, however, and the remainder of this section is concerned with how we can monitor or control the processes of change for any form of text file.

10.2.1   Formal control of change to a text file

For the individual worker, or the small team of specialists who may be working together on a scientific or technical project, any updating of programs or documents is likely to need little or no formal control and may be handled as individual responsibility or by consensus. Where the amount of software involved becomes larger and where a team of programmers may be cooperating in the construction of large software-based systems, then some formal method of requesting, making and recording changes usually becomes necessary, if only because of possible cross-effects where dependencies exist between different parts of the software.

The lack of version numbering for filenames has been mentioned, and in Chapter 9 a simple method for providing backup copies of files was demonstrated using shell programming methods. While a large project might find it sufficient to construct more powerful variants on this theme, it should be noted that a much more comprehensive scheme for controlling and recording changes to software is available as a part of the *Programmer's Workbench* package, which is additional to UNIX V7. (This particular item is an integral part of System V.)

The SCCS (Source Code Control System) maintains files by storing a **base version** of each file, and then recording all subsequent changes that are made to it as a series of **deltas**. Each delta contains the appropriate editing commands to reproduce the changes involved between two versions of a file, and to provide the user with any particular version, the SCCS system begins from the original form and simply applies the appropriate sequence of deltas to it. It also performs checks in order to ensure that the user is entitled to obtain a copy of the file, and to ensure that any new delta being generated is from a suitably authorised user. Since it is not a standard item for UNIX V7, a fuller description of SCCS is not appropriate at this point, although a few points about its use are so. SCCS can maintain **tree** structures of deltas. This allows a particular version to be fixed as an **issue** and then subsequent deltas either to lie on the path of producing the next issue or to lie on the path of modifications to that particular issue. Thus one path is concerned with producing a new form of the software, and the other simply with maintaining the current form. The use of SCCS applies to any form of text file, and so it provides an appropriate method for controlling the production of documents as well as of programs. There is no real point in SCCS maintaining binary files, since these can be regenerated at any time using the appropriate set of source files.

10.2.2   File security—the use of encryption

In describing the general filestore handling of UNIX in Chapter 4, a reference to the role of the **super-user** was included, together with an introduction to the concept of **access permission** forms that different classes of user could have to any particular file.

No computer system can be wholly secure to the extent that any user can be one hundred per cent confident that no other person can examine the contents of their share of the filestore. While UNIX is certainly far from being an insecure system in this sense when it is used correctly, it is as open as any other operating system to abuse of the powers of the super-user; and hence there is a particular need for those users who have privileged access via this facility to be especially careful that no-one else obtains their password. The encryption scheme used to store user passwords is a formidable defence, but only if the password is chosen with care. Using one's first name, or part of one's address, etc., is rarely prudent in that these will be the first things tried by the ill-intentioned or curious. (Deliberate mis-spellings also help here by randomising the chosen password very well!)

The user does however have one means of protecting a text file in a particularly effective manner. The utility program which encrypts passwords can also be used to encrypt (and decrypt) a complete file in the same manner, using a 'key' given by the user. By coupling this *crypt* utility program to any consumer programs (compilers, text formatters, etc.) via a pipe, we can ensure that at no time does a permanent copy of a readable form of the file need to exist on the system. (*crypt* is of course working in reverse when used in this way, and decoding the file from its encrypted form.) The processing overhead of using *crypt* is relatively small—and no-one, including the super-user, can decode a file if they do not have the necessary key.

There is however one slight sting in the tail. One facility that the super-user provision normally gives to us is the existence of a means of resetting a password that has been forgotten by its owner, in order to allow a user access to his files. This is simply done by the super-user modifying the appropriate entry in the file

```
/etc/passwd
```

or even by using the *passwd* utility itself, since the super-user does not need to know the old version. Encryption of files is a personal thing though, and the key is not stored in any way on the system—so if it is forgotten then the contents of the file are lost. So keep encryption for essential use only, and choose the key with care.

10.3 Handling source code files

Since this formed the subject matter for much of Part I, and Section 10.2 has already mentioned some general points about a utility system such as SCCS, which can be useful when handling source code files, this section is limited to making only one point on this topic; one which largely ties in with the general documentation theme of the chapter.

Every programmer knows that comments within a program are a 'good thing'—and some of them even put the odd one into their own programs to show this! There is no doubt that much of the code generated by programmers is generally inadequately provided with comments, and also that those comments provided may not always be particularly relevant either.

In trying to understand the workings of a program written by someone else, comments are obviously an important aid. As a means towards making constructive use of the comment facility of any language, it is a good idea to try and establish a personal or communal standard for comment layout, including such matters as form, style and purpose. A particular form that is found especially useful by some experienced programmers is to use a standard format of header comment block, listing various details about a program file, purpose, history, place of storage, name of the programmer who created it, etc. If this can be in a standard form, then so much the better.

Unfortunately, as most programmers prefer writing code to comments, to maintain such a standard is difficult, and it helps if some means can be found to provide the programmer with an easily used *aide-mémoire*. One method for doing this is to use a **pro-forma** comment generator. This is an interactive program which helps the programmer create the initial file, prompting for information under the standard headings and formatting the comment block appropriately. At the end of the session the normal text editor can be called up so that the user can proceed to enter his code as usual, following the comment block just created at the head of the file.

This is an ideal task for the use of shell programming facilities, and Fig. 10.1 shows an example of such a pro-forma, used in this case to generate comments for programs written in either Pascal or Modula-2. (The source language is relevant in that we need to provide the appropriate form of comment delimiters, and possibly some additional headings where separate or independent compilation is used.) The example of Fig. 10.1 uses standard *shell* utility programs, except for the 'insert' program which is used to copy the programmer's responses into the program file. The code (in C) for this program was given in Fig. 6.1. Figure 10.2 shows an example of the output form that is generated by using this particular pro-forma.

The use of such a tool is flexible, and it can be easily tailored to any preferred language and choice of prompts. Note too that not all of the information included is obtained from the user; such items as the date and the filename can be obtained directly from the system, thus reducing error, and some of the headings are included for later use when the file is updated. In an ideal system, the updating software would force the use of such headings—but devising the means for this is left as an exercise for the reader!

10.4 Documentation in general

The ability of a computer system to store and retrieve large quantities of information quickly makes it well suited to the storage and retrieval of many classes of documents. However, computers cannot search effectively without very clear directions, and so only

```
..      An example of a shell program used to create a comment pro-forma
..      for a Modula-2 program or a Pascal program
..      and in the process to open up the new file to be used.
..
echo "Pro-forma for Modula-2/Pascal"
echo
if test -f $1
then
        echo    "file already exists"
else
..      create new file with this block at start
..
..      explain format of input blocks to user
echo "end input text blocks with a line containing only a period"
echo
..      begin comment block in file and then conduct dialogue
echo "  (*" >$1
echo >>$1
echo "1. Project Title " >>$1
echo    "enter Project title"
iblock >>$1
echo >>$1
echo "2. Module Title " >>$1
echo "enter Module title"
iblock >>$1
echo >>$1
echo "3. Description of Module " >>$1
echo "describe Module"
iblock >>$1
echo >>$1
..
```

```
echo -n "4. Stored in    "  >>$1
echo -n $HOME >>$1
echo -n "/" >>$1
echo $1 >>$1
echo >>$1
echo "5. Version         0.0" >>$1
echo >>$1
echo -n "6. Created on   " >>$1
date >>$1
echo >>$1
echo "7. Updates -- date and nature  " >>$1
echo >>$1
echo "8. Definition modules required. " >>$1
echo "list Definition modules required"
iblock >>$1
echo >>$1
echo "9. Test routines or modules used with this module: " >>$1
echo "list any test routines for this module"
iblock >>$1
echo >>$1
echo "10. Comments: " >>$1
echo "enter any comments on module"
iblock >>$1
echo >>$1
echo -n "11. Author: " >>$1
echo "input your name"
iblock >>$1
echo >>$1
echo -n "12. Language: " >>$1
echo "Modula-2 or Pascal?"
iblock >>$1
echo    >>$1
echo    "          *)" >>$1
ed $1
fi
```

Fig. 10.1 An example pro-forma

```
            (*

1. Project Title:
        Making use of UNIX

2. Module Title:
        An example of proforma usage
        for Chapter 10.

3. Description of Module:
        Does very little in this case

4. Stored in:    /staff/db/test.m

5. Version       0.0

6. Created on:   Thu Apr 26 10:39:36 GMT 1984

7. Updates - date and nature:

8. Definition modules required:
        None

9. Test routines or modules used with this module:
        The reader's eagle eye

10. Comments:
        A very simple one

11. Author:     D Budgen

12. Language:   Pascal


    *)
```

Fig. 10.2 A typical header block using the pro-forma

those documents that fit under well-defined headings are really suitable, As a rule of thumb, if you wouldn't know clearly where a document was to be filed in a manual filing system, it would be very hard to retrieve it on a computerised system. One cannot rummage in filestore in the manner that is possible in a filing cabinet! Since all but the most throw-away of programs require some form of documentation, varying from the short note to the full set of reference manuals, there are some obvious benefits from being able to store these supporting documents alongside the programs that they describe.

   Like programs, documents need to be created, modified and even processed in various ways. So some supporting tools are needed at least to give the user the means to:

create and modify document files;
check documents for grammatical errors;
format them for printing;
record changes made to documents;
index documents and their contents.

The rest of this chapter is concerned with the first three points; and primarily with the third. Recording changes made to files requires a system such as SCCS, while indexing requires that the user make sensible use of file naming conventions and of subdirectories. However, UNIX is an excellent tool building system, and so any user is able to experiment with automating these last two items in a number of ways.

10.4.1 Creating and modifying documents

Since document files and source files are only distinguished by usage, their creation and modification can be performed using the same tools; chiefly the text editor utility. For the programmer this is an attraction, since documents can be handled using familiar facilities and without having to learn anything new. Where clerks or typists might be enlisted to assist with document preparation, it is likely that *ed* will be found rather unsuitable—and the attractions of screen editor programs will become only too apparent!

10.4.2 Checking documents

Storing a document in the filestore makes it possible to use the text editing and formatting programs, and also the range of pattern matching utilities that UNIX has to offer. For document handling, by far the most invaluable of those available is the *spell* utility program.

spell will scan through a file of text and match each word it finds against its 'dictionary' file, finally printing out an alphabetically ordered list of those words that it was unable to recognise. Its use is simple enough, as in the example below, where we enter

```
$ spell mydoc.2
etner
finaly
$
```

Here the user has directed *spell* to check the text file 'mydoc.2', and *spell* has reported two mis-spelt words within this file: one is caused by character reversal, and the other by a missing letter.

Dictionaries are available for both British and American spellings of the English language; the appropriate one is set as a local default, while the other can be selected via an option. The support program *spellin* permits a privileged user such as the super-user to add new words to the dictionary. This is mainly used so that locally used technical terms, names, addresses, etc., can be added, to reduce the spurious rejection of these by *spell*.

spell will recognise most derivations of a word, but it cannot pick up grammatical slips or errors that result in correct words in the wrong place. For example, we might mis-type

```
is is
```

instead of the intended

```
it is
```

Most users regard this remaining task of proof-reading as a small price to pay for the other benefits. Two hints when using *spell* are to apply it to the file after making corrections, as a check; and to remember to use the editor's search facility to ensure that a given error has not been repeated within a file.

spell (rather sneakily) maintains a 'history' file, in which the identity of the user (unfair), the date and time it was used, and a list of the errors found (embarrassing) are stored each time it runs. The object of this is to allow us to make an occasional survey of the resulting file in order to identify any terms or words that are in frequent local use and which might be usefully added to the dictionary file. This file should be cleared out from time-to-time to avoid its eventual occupation of the whole filestore!

A number of other utility programs are available and extract information from a file, rather than checking it in any particular way. *pubindex* takes a set of bibliographical references (i.e. details about books) and makes an index file which can then act as a source for the *refer* utility. *refer* in turn goes through a document, replacing abbreviated references with their full form. It does not necessarily need the output from *pubindex* in order to do this, but the form of the index file that is generated by *pubindex* makes *refer* run more efficiently. Finally, the *lookbib* program searches a bibliographic database created by the user for any matches to keywords that are given as its inputs, and produces a list of references as its output.

10.4.3   Text processing and formatting—the *roff* family

When thinking about text processing on UNIX, it is the *roff* programs that usually come to mind: *roff, nroff* and *troff*. The most simple in terms of facilities and ease of use is *roff*: this has now reached a frozen state, i.e. there is no further development planned for it. *nroff* and *troff* are twin programs which have taken the ideas of *roff* and expanded them further. *nroff* is used to drive standard character-oriented devices such as printers, while *troff* performs the same functions for a photo-typesetter which is capable of producing different type fonts and sizes. Given that few users are likely to have one of these to hand, the following discussion will be confined to *roff* and *nroff*, although most references to the latter can be understood to include *troff* too.

What sort of processing of a text file do we expect to obtain from this type of program? In general the aim is to improve the layout of the text, and to save the user time and effort spent in trying to input text in a particular format. In addition, we can adjust or modify the layout at any time simply by changing some of the embedded commands to the text formatting program. Most important of all, we can insert new chunks of text, and delete text, without concerning ourselves with the effects upon the final printed format.

The facilities of such a formatting program will usually include:

(i)   provision of right justification of text, i.e. the right-hand margin of the page will be aligned to form a straight edge;
(ii)   page numbering, so that if we insert or delete text, the pages will automatically be re-numbered for us;
(iii) printing of page headers at the top of each page;
(iv)   printing of footnotes;

(v)   indentation of the margins to give emphasis to blocks of text;
(vi)   selective underlining of words and phrases.

The commands for these will normally be inserted into the normal text of the file, and will be distinguished by the use of a special character.

All of these features and more are provided by the *roff* family. *roff* itself is fairly simple to use, and its execution is quick and efficient. The commands that can be embedded in the text to control the formatting are all concerned with straightforward tasks; i.e. they perform a single action such as indenting the margin by so many spaces, or underlining the following line of text. For many forms of document preparation, *roff* is the easiest way to obtain the required effects.

Where more elaborate formats are involved, and particularly where this involves the preparation of technical papers with footnotes, an abstract, an index, paragraph numbering, etc., *nroff* has a wider set of appropriate commands as well as a set of formatting macros for such use. In addition there are some specialist pre-processor programs available for use in conjunction with *nroff*, and which provide for the handling of the layout of tables and the formatting of mathematical expressions. The *tbl* utility allows the user to design a table format, while *neqn* enables us to format mathematical expressions. They each produce as output a mix of *nroff* directives in the original text, and so can be connected directly to the standard input of *nroff* via the pipe mechanism. For example, the command

```
$ tbl  mydoc.t  |  nroff  >mytable
```

causes *tbl* to process the commands and text stored in 'mydoc.t', and to pass its output to *nroff* which formats the table as required. The final formatted output is then stored in the file 'mytable'.

The rest of this chapter gives some introductory examples of the use of these programs, and some hints on how they might be most effectively managed and used.

Printing devices
For a text formatting program to be able to produce correctly aligned outputs, it needs to know the size of page that will be used as well as the characteristics of the printer. The most common typefaces in use have either ten characters to the inch or twelve characters to the inch, and in normal spacing mode will print six lines to the inch vertically. For fanfold line printer paper, the normal length (form size) is eleven inches, although many other sizes are available. As defaults, the *roff* programs assume that the printer has the larger of these two typefaces, i.e. ten characters to the inch; and so set the default line length for the output to be 65 characters, although this may easily be changed. Similarly the page length is assumed to be 66 lines, for use with an eleven inch form length of paper.

When using a high quality printer such as a daisy-wheel, we can often use standard document paper sizes such as A4. In such a case, we simply change the page length to match. Similarly we may lengthen the line length using the appropriate command, if the typeface is twelve characters to the inch. One inconvenience of making such changes is that it is often convenient when producing documents in this way if we can print out proof copies on a faster printer, such as a line printer or dot matrix printer. Such printers often use a different page size or line length. One fairly simple (and typically UNIX) solution is to leave the page length defaults unchanged within the text formatting, and to run the output to the printer via a shell program that adds a few blank lines on each page if the longer form paper is being used. This way we waste some of the space on our larger pages, but the pagination remains consistent. Alternatively we can print out with the page length reset to the longer size, and output pages will then be offset from the shorter line printer pages.

Command formats

The commands that control the actions of *roff* and *nroff* are inserted into the raw text of the document, one command per line, and are preceded by the period character '.' to indicate that this line contains a formatting command rather than text. The commands concerned with the physical layout of the output on the page need some form of parameter in order to indicate the degree of change required. This can be given as an unsigned number, to indicate a new value; for example (for *roff*):

    .pl 72

This sets the value for the output page length to be 72 lines. Alternatively, it may be given as a signed number, to indicate a relative change; for example:

    .pl +6

This indicates that the value currently being used for the page length should be increased by six. Items such as the level of margin indentation, which change quite frequently, are usually better expressed as relative changes, whereas such parameters as the page length, which is set once at the beginning, might be more conveniently expressed as an absolute value.

An important concept used in formatting text with these programs is that of the **break**. A break indicates to the text processor that it should include a newline character in the output at that point, regardless of whether or not it has completed a line, and so stops the 'filling' of the current line being output. (**Filling** is the action of packing out the line with extra spaces in order to keep the right margin even.) Some commands automatically involve a break.

You should note that the *spell* utility will normally ignore any *roff* or *nroff* commands that it encounters in a file, and can therefore be used on a file of raw text which still contains formatting commands. This is better than using it on the formatted file, especially if the latter uses hyphenation (see p. 135) since *spell* sometimes has trouble with hyphenated words. In addition, note that the single quote, '''', has special effects if it appears as the first character of a line. To disable this effect, it must be quoted with the usual '\' character.

A few hints on using roff *and* nroff

As with all such programs, it helps to develop a few personal conventions to ensure consistent style and use, and the following points might help in selecting such conventions.

Unless the appropriate option is specifically disabled, the *roff* programs will try to 'fill' each line of output in order to maintain nicely aligned right margins on the output. The 'filling' is achieved by adding extra spaces between words along the line and by hyphenating longer words that occur at the end of lines. By default, both programs will hyphenate words, and while this is fairly effective, the choice of division is sometimes a little odd.

Unless the output format requires the use of very narrow columns, there will be relatively little distortion in the final appearance of the text if the hyphenation option is disabled; in this case the processor has to 'fill' purely by adding extra spaces. Since the hyphenation is sometimes rather unconventional, the result is generally rather easier to read if it is turned off.

The preparation of a document is also largely a matter of preference, which may change with increasing experience of use. Some users enter the raw text into a file and then insert the formatting commands, while others include them as they enter the text. It may be easier to insert commands such as the underline with the text, especially where individual words need to be highlighted in this way. Format control commands such as indentation may be better added later, since it is fairly easy to lose track of current level of indentation over a long text.

Many documents fall into a number of sections, which might or might not be numbered. To simplify document maintenance and handling in general, it is a useful idea to keep each section in a separate file, and use the *shell* facilities to merge them on input to the text formatter. As an example, if our document has been divided into four parts, then it might be stored in the files

```
mydoc.1, mydoc.2, mydoc.3, mydoc.4
```

These can then be processed by a command such as

```
$ roff  mydoc.[1-4]  >finalversion
```

or

```
$ nroff  mydoc.[1-4]  >finalversion
```

as appropriate. Note that any defaults set up in the first file for the page length, width, etc., will be carried through the whole of the final document; *roff* and *nroff* will process the four files as though they were a single concatenated input.

In even larger documents, perhaps split into chapters which are in turn split into sections, the same method applies and we choose a file naming convention that allows the main part of the filename to indicate the chapter too. It is also a useful practice to number the pages according to the chapter, so that a change within one chapter does not require us to reprint all the later ones purely to accommodate a page numbering change. A scheme of page numbering such as

```
1-1 , 1-2 , 1-3 , ... , 1-15 , 2-1 , 2-2 ...
```

is easily generated by the *roff* 'header' command using a form such as

```
.he '''page 2-%'
```

where the '%' will be replaced by the appropriate page number on each page, so allowing the paging to be easily maintained by the processing system.

Both of the *roff* programs allow us to select a group of pages for the output. The command

```
$ roff  +31  mydoc.[1-4]  >lastpart
```

or its equivalent

```
$ nroff  -o31-  mydoc.[1-4]  >lastpart
```

will output pages 31 to the end of 'mydoc' into the file 'lastpart', and similarly the command

```
$ roff  -6  mydoc.[1-4]  >firstpart
```

or,

```
$ nroff -o-6  mydoc.[1-4] >firstpart
```

will output the first six pages of 'mydoc' into the file 'firstpart'. We can of course combine these too, in order to select a group of pages from the middle of the document; for example

```
$ roff  +6 -10  mydoc.[1-4]  >middlepart
```

or either of the equivalent forms for *nroff*:

```
$ nroff  -o6-10  mydoc.[1-4]  >middlepart
```

or

```
$ nroff  -o6,7,8,9,10  mydoc.[1-4]  >middlepart
```

These will place pages 6 to 10 inclusive into the file 'middlepart'. Note that here all reference to 'pages' means those imposed by the text processing. This option is very useful whenever we have made some changes which have not affected the overall pagination, or have only affected the latter part of the file, and so we need only reprint a selected part of the document.

Examples of roff

roff is described here in a little more detail because it is the simpler to use, and hence provides a better demonstration of the techniques available. Most of the *roff* commands are identical with those used by *nroff*, although the parameters may differ a little; the only one in the list below that differs significantly is the .he command. The differences are described later.

All of the *roff* commands consist of the period character '.', followed by two lower-case letters, and occupying a single line. Figure 10.3 shows an example of a raw file to be input to *roff*, with the commands interspersed in the text, while Fig. 10.4 shows the output that will be produced by processing this file. Most of the commands used in this example are generally useful, and a group that are worth describing individually is a follows.

.ll   Used to increase or reduce the line width. In the example of Fig. 10.3, the printer being used has a typeface of twelve characters to the inch, and so the line length has been increased by ten characters since we can print more characters in the given page width.

.po   This command causes the given number of spaces (in this case ten) to be added at the beginning of each line of output to provide a left margin. It is useful when printing, but can be a nuisance when proof-reading on a VDU screen if the screen is too narrow to hold the full line width generated.

.he   (Not available in *nroff*)   This specifies the header titles to be printed at the top of each page (if any), at the left corner, the centre and the right corner. In the example we have used the centre and the right corner only. Note that when used inside these title fields, the '%' character will be replaced by the appropriate page number for each page of output.

.hy Controls hyphenation. The default parameter is 1, which sets hyphenation to 'on'. In the example it has been turned 'off' in the middle of the text in order to demonstrate the difference. Normally of course this would be selected at the beginning of the file if no hyphenation was required.

.ul Causes the following *n* lines to be underlined, where *n* is the unsigned parameter. Since it does not cause a break it can be used to underline individual words as shown. Since spaces along a line are not underlined, to obtain continuous underlining of titles, etc., we use the underscore character in place of the space.

.in This command controls indentation of the left margin. To indent the right margin, we need to use .ll. Indentation is a good means of making a block of text stand out to the eye. There are two forms; .in causes a break to occur while .ix does not. Additionally, .ti simply indents an individual line.

.nf Stops the processor 'filling' output lines, i.e. leaves the text 'raw'.

.fi Starts the filling of lines, i.e. reverses the effect of .nf.

.ne The argument *n* is used to direct the text processor to check whether it can fit the following *n* lines of output onto the present page. If not, then the page is filled out with empty lines and the output is begun on the next page. This is a good means of keeping examples or other blocks of text intact.

This group of commands should be quite enough to enable a user to get underway with *roff*. The use of other commands (such as **.ce** to centre lines on the page), particularly those that organise page headers and footnotes, can be mastered as the need arises.

Where we may be using a standardised layout for a number of entries in a document (or even for a number of documents), *roff* provides a simple form of local **macro** facility. A macro definition begins with a **.de** command, and ends with a line containing only '..'. Macros defined in this way cannot have parameters, but can still be very useful for certain classes of document. As an example, the macro definition given by:

```
.de my
.in +4
.ds
.nf
..
```

has the effect of indenting the lines that follow the command .my by four spaces, printing them double-spaced and with no filling. Similarly, the macro defined by:

```
.de yo
.in -4
.ls 1
.fi
..
```

tells the text processor to reverse these changes: returning the margin out again by four spaces, returning to single spaced lines and filling the output again. In use they might be called in:

```
.my
< lines of text >
.yo
```

in the same way that we use the standard *roff* commands.

```
.ll +4
.he ''A roff demonstration'page -%-'
.pl 30

.ce
.ul 1
An_example_of_the_use_of_roff

.ul 1
Introduction

.in +4
This is a demonstration piece of text to show how we can make use of roff
to produce nicely formatted output. Note that this section is produced with
the hyphenation option set to value '1', and hence if we are using long enough
words then hyphenation of words will
occur at the end of some lines.

For a new paragraph, just force a line break by entering a blank line between
two lines in this way. Some of the option are often used in groups, for example
the next few lines need to be kept together, and so not only are they included in
a 'raw' form, but also the '.ne' option is used to ensure that no page throw
appears in the middle.

.ne 6
.nf
.in +4
This part is entered in a 'raw' form, it
is mostly useful for producing examples
or where the format of a program needs to
be kept unchanged (i.e. the lines are not
```

```
to be 'filled'). These lines have not
been 'filled' because of this.
.fi
.in -4

.ne 6
.ul 1
Hyphenation

.hy 0
This part of the file is output using no hyphenation so the lines are sometimes a
little stretched because the text processor pads them out with extra spaces.
With a little practice it is fairly easy to insert the formatting commands as
the user goes along, entering text and commands within the same editing session.
The next command writes an intended title line and then keeps ten
lines free for a diagram.

.ne 14
.ti +6
This could be a title for the diagram
.sp 10
Obviously
there are many interesting effects that can be produced with this scheme, we
can emphasise certain words by
.ul 1
underlining
them in the middle of the text, though of course we cannot change the type
font itself in any way.
.in -4
```

Fig. 10.3 An example of an input file for *roff*

A roff demonstration   page -1-

An example of the use of roff

Introduction

This is a demonstration piece of text to show how we can make use of roff to produce nicely formatted output. Note that this section is produced with the hyphenation option set to value '1', and hence if we are using long enough words then hyphenation of words will occur at the end of some lines.

For a new paragraph, just force a line break by entering a blank line between two lines in this way. Some of the option are often used in groups, for example the next few lines need to be kept together, and so not only are they included in a 'raw' form, but also the '.ne' option is used to ensure that no page throw appears in the middle.

A roff demonstration   page -2-

This part is entered in a 'raw' form, it is mostly useful for producing examples or where the format of a program needs to be kept unchanged (i.e. the lines are not to be 'filled'). These lines have not been 'filled' because of this.

<u>Hyphenation</u>

This part of the file is output using no hyphenation so the lines are sometimes a little stretched because the text processor pads them out with extra spaces. With a little practice it is fairly easy to insert the formatting commands as the user goes along, entering text and commands within the same editing session. The next command writes an intended title line and then keeps ten lines free for a diagram.

A roff demonstration   page -3-

This could be a title for the diagram

Obviously there are many interesting effects that can be produced with this scheme, we can emphasise certain words by <u>underlining</u> them in the middle of the text, though of course we cannot change the type font itself in any way.

Fig. 10.4 A sample of the output produced by *roff*

When using both *roff* and *nroff* you should note that although commands are normally denoted by the period '.' at the beginning of a line, we can change this **command character** using the **.cc** command if we wish to be able to use the period itself. In the example below it is changed to the '#' character for the purpose, and is then returned to being the period again after the particular lines have been printed:

```
.cc #
#nf
.text is used for code
.data is used for variables
#fi
#cc .
```

A useful facility when producing an example of how to use *roff*!

nroff—*some differences*

While many of the *nroff* command formats will be familiar to a user of *roff*, there are many extensions and additions available in terms of formats and powerful facilities. As an example of this, with *roff* the parameters of a command such as .po, used to set a margin, or .ll, used to change the line width, have to be given in units of characters. With *nroff* the parameters for the equivalent commands can be given using a number of base units including characters, centimetres, inches, or ens (a printer's measure).

One feature of *nroff* that requires rather more work from the user is in setting up titles to be placed at the head or foot of every page. *roff* provides commands such as .he for this, while for *nroff* the user must use the pagination control more directly; however, it is straightforward to set up macros to emulate the facilities of commands such as .he.

A particular attraction of *nroff*, apart from its ability to take inputs from *tbl* and *neqn*, is the '–ms' option that can be used for preparing technical documents. It has various macros that can be used to help in producing title pages, abstract pages, paragraph numbering schemes, etc., in the appropriate formats; these can be called up in the normal manner of formatting commands.

Figure 10.5 shows an example of a raw input file to be used with *nroff*, and which uses the '–ms' macros. These macros need to be specified as an option, as in the command

```
$ nroff -ms mytext.1
```

Forgetting to do so produces some odd results.

Figure 10.6 shows a part of the output generated from Fig. 10.5, with the page size reduced considerably in order to show the effects more fully. Note that the macros are distinguished by the use of upper-case characters for their names; standard *nroff* commands use lower-case characters. As with *roff*, all commands occupy a single line and begin with the period character.

nroff and *roff* will both ignore any unrecognised commands that they encounter in their inputs, and do not issue any form of error message to indicate that they have found anything untoward at any point.

10.4.4 Text processing—a conclusion

The *roff* text processing programs offer a powerful facility to aid the programmer in preparing and producing documents on the UNIX system. Indeed the UNIX manuals

```
.nr LL 7i
.nr PO 0.5i
.RP
.TL
This is the title line
.AU
And the author : D Budgen
.AI
The affiliation : University of Stirling
.AB
This is the 'abstract' block that will be printed in a narrower
column width than the rest of the article and which will appear on
a separate page of the text together with the title and the
author's name.
.AE
.SH
A sub-title
.LP
Each new paragraph begins with the 'LP' macro if no indentation is
to be used. Note that the upper-case letters are macro calls and the
lower-case letters '.nr' refer to direct nroff calls to change a parameter
used by nroff (in this case the default line length and the default page
offset).
.LP
Another paragraph.  The nroff format does not make the input file particularly
readable, but it does produce a very neat layout on output. Note that the
defaults for such parameters as page length, line length and offset can be
modified by specifying the changes using various default units (inches, ems,
centimetres), and as relative or absolute values. Of course, the calculation
that nroff makes, will assume a particular character size on the printer.
In the first two lines, the values of line length and page offset (margin)
are specified using units of inches.
```

Fig. 10.5   An example of an input file for *nroff* (with -ms macros)

This is the title line

And the author : D Budgen

The affiliation : University of Stirling

ABSTRACT

This is the 'abstract' block that will be printed   in
a   narrower   column width than the rest of the article and
which will appear on a separate page of the text   together
with the title and the author's name.

May 6, 1984

This is the title line

And the author : D Budgen

The affiliation : University of Stirling

<u>A sub-title</u>

Each new paragraph begins with the 'LP' macro if no indentation is   to
be   used.   Note   that   the upper-case letters are macro calls and the
lower-case letters '.nr' refer to   direct   nroff   calls   to   change   a
parameter   used by nroff (in this case the default line length and the
default page offset).

Another paragraph. The nroff format does not make the input file particularly   readable, but it does produce a very neat layout on output.
Note that the defaults for such parameters as page length, line length
and   offset   can   be   modified by specifying the changes using various
default units (inches, ems, centimetres), and as relative or   absolute
values.   Of   course,   the calculation that nroff makes, will assume a
particular character size on the printer.   In the first two lines, the
values   of   line   length   and page offset (margin) are specified using
units of inches.

May 6, 1984

Fig. 10.6   An example of *nroff* output

and guides are produced via *nroff* and *troff*; hence the ability to provide a facility such as the *man* utility, which simply runs the appropriate file through *nroff* and out to the user's screen. However, it is the combination of the *roff*s with the other features of UNIX that makes them particularly significant as software tools. The ability to organise files in subdirectories in a simple manner, and to combine files using the *shell* facilities, the freedom to use file naming conventions that suit one's own needs, and to use supporting programs such as *tbl*; these features add the special UNIX flavour to the business of text processing. The *roff*s are quite addictive, but this is usually beneficial in that it is likely to result in improved standards and quantities of program documentation and, dare one suggest, documentation where otherwise there would be no documentation at all.

For the production of well-engineered software we need to recognise that a programmer's time is only partly spent upon the task of writing code. Of the other tasks involved in the engineering process, documentation is an especially significant one, and the UNIX facility for integrating text processing into the system so well can only be an advantage in aiding the production of well-documented work. It is this integration of software methodology and technique that allows even the beginner on a UNIX system to be able to handle text processing with only a small learning overhead.

11
Management and communication on the UNIX system

11.1 Management of what, by whom?

In one sense all programmers are managers too, since each is responsible for the use and housekeeping of their own part of the filestore. So while many of the ideas of this chapter are concerned with utility programs that are particularly of interest to those programmers who work as members of a group, and perhaps supervise the work of others too, there are many that are also useful to the individual user who is pursuing his own work with little or no reference to any other users of the system.

As to the question of what it is that is being managed, the answer to this is 'resources'. The filestore is one obvious example of a resource that may need managing in some way, particularly where several programmers may share access to the contents of a directory. For larger teams of workers, whether professional programmers working together to produce a large software-based system, or research workers needing to interchange data and information, other shared facilities and objectives may require the exercise of some form of control. The interfaces between program modules, data formats, file access, software changes, quality control, etc., may all require some sort of coordination and communication between the individual workers involved.

11.2 A software development philosophy

Anyone who has tried to work with someone else to develop a program will be only too well aware of the need to establish firm standards for the interfaces between the different parts of the program, as well as the need to have some means of ensuring that everyone is aware when any changes occur that may affect them. If these points are not organised, then the ensuing problems can quickly become far more time-consuming than the actual programming task itself. Local standards need to be established at the outset, and maintained throughout the work. This is not so easy in practice of course, especially as maintaining the standards concerned is largely a matter requiring personal discipline from each programmer. The operating system can rarely offer much assistance in enforcing such standards, and UNIX is no different to any others in this particular respect. However, we can exploit the facilities of UNIX in order to make some of the tasks easier for the programmer, and do so simply by writing a few simple shell programs, as the rest of this section will demonstrate.

At this point it is helpful to assess what sort of facilities a manager of a team of programmers might find helpful. (The manager may be a professional software manager, or simply the senior member of a research team, depending on the form of the group and its purpose.) Some needs that can be identified include the following:

(i)   keeping a 'history' of the development of each item of software, so that past versions of source files and documents can be retrieved;
(ii) recording the details and results of any tests performed on each item of software;

(iii) controlling programmer access to source files and document files, so that only those so authorised may make changes to them;

(iv) exercising some form of quality control over all of the code and documentation produced;

(v) monitoring the progress of the software development, and assessing its current state at any point during development.

These points may be considered to sum up the major problems of software engineering too!

11.2.1 Maintaining a history of software development

A good start point is to question whether such a record is needed or not. In the commercial sphere, where a programming team may need to maintain several operational versions of complex software at any given time, then the answer must be 'yes'. In such cases the UNIX V7 system alone is not enough, and the SCCS facility becomes essential.

In other situations, the need may be harder to define, and the conclusions of Chapter 9 that one level of backup is sufficient protection may be quite enough to provide an insurance against most accidents. Recording the key points that occur during development may require little more than a notebook and pencil, although some of the following examples suggest ways of maintaining this information in a log file on the machine.

11.2.2 Recording tests

Dynamic testing of software usually involves running a program, or part of a program, while using test data to exercise its functions. The outputs produced are then analysed to see if they agree with our predicted outputs; if not, then we must decide whether the program or the predictions are in error.

When developing a single program, even one which is large enough to possess well-defined sub-functions that can be separately developed and tested, the simple methods outlined in Chapter 9 should suffice for our needs. The records required in such cases are the files containing test data together with copies of the outputs produced; the latter might well be conveniently kept only in printed form.

For larger systems, and large programs, organising and performing any degree of rigorous testing rapidly increases in complexity, and hence in the amount of time required for it. Each module may need to be tested in isolation, and then again after being integrated with the rest of the program. Organisationally we can assist in this by grouping together all of the files needed to construct a single module in one subdirectory, so that any programmer working on a module can have all of the appropriate source files, binary files and test data files immediately available.

Keeping records of such work cannot easily be delegated to the machine in any way, though we can insert appropriate *echo* messages to update a log file within any command files used to reconstruct our program(s). Another possible aid to record-keeping might be to use another pro-forma, rather like that used in Fig. 10.1. Such a device could aid the programmer in updating the log file manually, and might even be run as a part of the logging off sequence. Figure 11.1 suggests a possible form for such a facility, written as a shell program, and Fig. 11.2 shows a typical entry that might be generated with its aid.

```
: a shell program to act as a pro-forma for maintaining a test log
: for a project.  To be used before logging out or on completion of
: an item of work
:
echo "Update for module testing log files"
echo
:
: set entry data and module name
:
echo -n "Test update entry on " >>$1
date >>$1
echo >>$1
echo "Module tested:" >>$1
echo >>$1
echo "Which module was tested ?"
iblock >>$1
echo >>$1
:
: specify the tested items and the test data
:
echo "Facilities exercised by test:" >>$1
echo >>$1
echo "Which features of the module were tested:"
iblock >>$1
echo >>$1
echo "Specific test data:" >>$1
echo >>$1
echo "Enter test data values, or data filename"
iblock >>$1
echo >>$1
:
: note results of test session
:
echo "Test results:" >>$1
echo >>$1
echo "What conclusions were reached ?"
iblock >>$1
echo >>$1
echo "Comments:" >>$1
echo >>$1
echo "Any further comments ?"
iblock >>$1
echo >>$1
: end of pro-forma
```

Fig. 11.1   A pro-forma for maintaining a test log

```
Test update entry on Fri May  6 13:46:25 GMT 1983
```

```
Module tested:
```

```
    First module
```

```
Facilities exercised by test:
```

```
    Inputs
```

```
Specific test data:
```

```
    All upper-case and lower-case characters
    and numeric characters too
```

```
Test results:
```

```
    It works for these
```

```
Comments:
```

```
    None
```

Fig. 11.2 Output produced from the test log pro-forma

11.2.3 Controlling access to files

Anyone using the SCCS facility has the protection of controlled access built in, but other users must find different means to protect their files. The most obvious method is to make use of the protection bits that are associated with every file and directory on the system. While the division of all users into the classes 'user', 'group' and 'world' is fairly coarse, it at least provides a first line of defence. Encryption might be acceptable for some cases, but if overused then its value rapidly declines as the keys used will become too widely known, and so will breach the protection provided.

The *chmod* utility used to change file protection does not have a particularly memorable format—and one way to encourage programmers to use it more often is to construct one or more shell programs that provide an easier interface. This might be done for other UNIX utilities too. The following shell program is a simple example of doing this, to be stored in the file 'meonly':

```
    : shell program to protect a file for access
    : by me only - stored in ´meonly´
    if test -s $1
    then
        chmod a-rwx $1
        chmod u+rx $1
    fi
```

This is simple enough, and we then need only type the command

```
$ meonly myprog
```

to ensure that only we can use and execute the file 'myprog'. Variants on this can easily be generated to suit particular needs; the next chapter suggests how it can take a more interactive form.

11.2.4 Quality control

Quality control is a rather nebulous concept for most programmers, associated rather more with manufactured goods than with software. However, the application of certain standards to a software product should be as important as for any other manufactured item. The UNIX system cannot actually enforce any standards of this type, but it can help us to generate standards, as well as performing some of the checking. Again, the facility we can most easily utilise for this is the pro-forma, used here to standardise our documentation layout and program comments. In the case of document files, the pro-forma can even insert the appropriate *roff* commands if necessary. Figure 11.3 gives a very simple example of how to do just this, while Fig. 11.4 shows an example of the sort of output that can be produced.

```
: a shell program to produce a standard document layout using
: the roff text formatting program.
: This routine inserts the basic set of roff commands for the
: appropriate printer and then invites the user to insert their
: text for the document.
:
: first parameter of call is the document title
: second parameter of call is the document filename
:
echo ".ll +8" >$2
echo ".po +8" >>$2
echo ".hy 0" >>$2
echo ".he ''"$1"'page -%-'" >>$2
echo "enter document title (one line)"
echo ".ce 1" >>$2
echo ".ul 1" >>$2
block >>$2
echo ".sp +4" >>$2
echo ".in +4" >>$2
echo "now enter text, separate paragraphs by blank lines"
block >>$2
echo "spelling check"
spell $2
echo "final output form"
roff $2
```

Fig. 11.3 A sample document pro-forma program

```
Example_document                                    page -1-
```

<u>This is an example of using a document generating pro-forma</u>

This is a simple example, intended to show how one can produce a fairly standard basic layout of document. If a document is intended to be structured into sections, then this can be fairly easily included in the structure of the pro-forma file.

Of course the normal 'roff' commands are still available, we can use the <u>underline</u> for individual words or phrases, and can
>   indent a block to make it stand out to the eye if we so wish.
>   However, for a fuller formatting, this would be better as a
>   feature that was directed by the pro-forma rather than by the
>   user.

A simple idea, but one that can obviously be extended to fit many forms of standard within an organisation - or even for a user's own purposes.

Fig. 11.4   Sample output from the document pro-forma

11.2.5 Monitoring progress

The adage that 'software is 90% complete for 90% of the time' is uncomfortably close to the truth for comfort, as many software producers and consumers will be only too well aware! Too often any estimates of the time and effort needed to produce a program seem to be based on hope rather than on history—and modelling techniques for making the estimates are still fairly unreliable—reflecting perhaps the significance of the human factor in the production of software. However, there are certain milestones which occur during the production of software, and which can be identified with some certainty and used as an aid to the recording of the development process. It is worth doing this, if only as an aid to future estimating. Some milestones we can use and identify include the following:

   (i)   completion of the specification for a module;
  (ii)   completion of the top-down design for a module;
 (iii)   completion of the detailed design for a module, i.e. all of the Structured English and the details of the data structures;
  (iv)   completion of initial coding of the module;
   (v)   completion of the module testing.

It is questionable whether integration testing is ever wholly completed, since every run of the software on real data can be thought of as being a test too.

These milestones can be roughly identified, even accepting that some of the processes involved are fairly iterative. We will probably make changes to all of the data involved at some later point, but at least the completion of the first pass can be identified fairly clearly. Unfortunately UNIX cannot contribute significantly to this. At best we can maintain a system log, and use the *date* utility to 'stamp' each use of it. The log might be updated each time we log on, or log off, or use a program such as the backup editor *eb*. However limited the information so gathered, it will at least enable us to maintain some record of development, although the specification and design stages can only be recorded by making a specific entry. A log file can be quite a useful aid when writing a final report, be it for internal or external consumption, since it is surprising how often we find that we have no real idea of how much time was used up in producing and testing an item of software.

11.2.6 Making use of *make*

The *make* utility was introduced in Chapter 9, together with a simple example of its use. While not the easiest of the utility programs to master, it is worth making the effort to do so since its use can aid the practices discussed in this chapter, particularly during the testing phases where we can so easily lose control of the situation.

Integration testing is a time when unstructured changes can only too easily occur to our programs—especially if we program at the terminal. It is easy to forget to recompile all of the parts of the program that may be affected by a change just made, perhaps those that depend upon a particular COMMON block or data structure. Using *make* to build our programs will at least ensure that each rebuild of a program will be consistent, and if we begin by recognising that a large program needs a stepwise development, then it will pay us to develop the 'makefile' along with the program itself. This will certainly prove easier than trying to put a 'makefile' together when the structure of the program has already become complex.

As a last hint, if we take the example of a 'makefile' that was given in Fig. 9.15, then by changing the last lines to the following we can ensure an automatic update of our log file whenever we rebuild:

```
variance:   main.o subs.o
            f77 main.o subs.o
            echo -n "variance rebuilt on " >>logfile
            date  >>logfile
```

11.3 Communication with others

UNIX provides two very useful means by which the users of the UNIX system can exchange messages with one another. The first is concerned with immediate messages, allowing two users to conduct a dialogue from their terminals; the second with a **mail** facility by which we can send a message to another user that will be stored and then 'delivered' to the recipient when he next logs on to the system.

11.3.1 Passing immediate messages

On some multi-user systems, asking another user a question may involve no more than turning one's head; on others we may have to climb stairs and travel corridors, since terminals can be located at quite large distances from the computer itself. Once a networking system is available then almost anything becomes possible in terms of configuration and distance.

The *write* utility enables any user to send a message to another active user at their terminal. *write* takes the message that is typed in on the standard input and outputs it to the recipient's screen, preceded by a 'tag' line which identifies the sender and their terminal. Since the message may be several lines long, the end of the input is signalled to *write* by an end-of-file on the standard input, produced by typing a control-Z character (or control-D on the Bell Laboratories version). At the recipient terminal, this will appear as the character string 'EOF'. As an example of doing this, suppose we are again logged on as 'NewUser'. If we are using the terminal 'ttyb', then to send a message to user 'fredb', currently logged on at terminal 'ttyf', we enter:

```
$ write fredb
What time is lunch today?
<control-Z>
$
```

On the terminal 'ttyf', the message will appear as:

```
Message from NewUser ttyb
What time is lunch today?
EOF
```

The message will break in to whatever other output may be currently appearing on 'ttyf' (if any).

The only option available with *write* is to include the identity of the recipient's terminal as a parameter following the name; this is useful where the recipient user may have logged on to more than one terminal for some reason. (We can obtain a list of users who are currently logged on, and their terminals, by using the *who* utility program.) So our command line to begin the above exercise would then look like:

```
$ write fredb ttyf
```

The output generated by *write* will break in to whatever other output is currently appearing on the user's screen. This is usually acceptable, but there are occasions when it would be inconvenient to have this sort of message appearing; for example, if we are printing out a table or displaying a graph on our screen. So there is a further utility program *mesg*, which can be used to set a terminal to 'accept' or 'refuse' such messages. It has only one parameter, which can take two possible values: 'y' to accept messages and 'n' to refuse them. The 'y' option is set as default when we first log on to a terminal.

As an example of this, we might use *mesg* in a sequence such as the following:

```
$ mesg n
< ....
 any other sequence of commands
 .... >
$ mesg y
```

This will 'bracket' the output that we wish to protect. Certain utility programs such as *nroff* will do this for themselves; and of course we can include *mesg* in any shell programs ourselves. Note that the super-user can break through this protection mechanism in order to send a message to any user. The super-user also has a broadcasting version of *write*, the *wall* utility, which sends the given message to all of the active terminals.

write can be used by a pair of users to conduct a dialogue, although it helps to have some form of 'over and out' convention to maintain control of it! A message is passed over line by line as it is entered and the end-of-file at the end is echoed as 'EOF' to the recipient.

11.3.2 The mailbox facility

The *mail* utility program provides a more general service than *write*, although the basic use is very similar. Sending a message via *mail* is much the same process as using *write*; we specify the recipient's identity (or identities; there can be more than one), and enter the message on the standard input, which can of course be taken from a file for either program. An example of doing this might be:

```
$ mail fredb
Could you please return my copy of the C manual
as I will be needing it next week?
<control-Z>
$
```

In the case of *mail*, the recipient user does not need to be currently logged on, since instead of displaying the message at once, it is stored instead in the recipient's 'mailbox'. This is a directory that is owned by the recipient, but which is only accessed indirectly via *mail* itself. When the recipient next logs on to the system, he will be informed that there is a message (or several messages) in the mailbox by the message

```
You have mail.
```

on his terminal screen.

To examine our mail, we type the command

```
$ mail
```

with no parameters. *mail* will then print out the contents of the first message on to our screen, and then prompt with a '?' character to request a directive. There are several directives that we can give to it, but the most immediately useful are as follows.

'return' *mail* keeps the message in the mailbox and goes on to print any following message. If there are no other messages then *mail* returns control to the *shell*.

d *mail* deletes the message just read, and goes on to display the next message, exiting if no others are available.

p *mail* prints the message again.

s buffer *mail* saves the message by copying it to the named file ('buffer') and then deletes it from the mailbox, continuing to the next message.

w buffer *mail* saves the original message in the named file, without the message header.

x *mail* exits to the *shell*, leaving the mailbox unchanged.

If any messages are left in the mailbox, then we will receive the prompting message again when we next log on, regardless of whether or not any new messages have been received.

The *mail* facility provides us with a very useful means of communicating information within a group of users, since it can be used to inform others of changes and events. In addition, if copying a file to someone else, it also enables us to transfer the ownership of the copy to the recipient—unlike *cp*. To aid its use within shell programs, the input to *mail* can optionally be terminated by a line containing only a period '.', instead of control-Z. A short shell program using this facility is given below as an example. This shell program, 'rebuild', is used to re-create a system, 'basesystem', and to inform a group of users whenever an update has been generated.

```
: simple shell routine to rebuild basesystem after
: a change and to inform the team
: stored in file group/rebuild
:
make basesystem
mail tomt billt lesw grouprecord
basesystem has been updated again
echo -n 'basesystem updated by' >>grouprecord
who am i >>grouprecord
```

This program also copies the message into the log file 'grouprecord', putting the current user's username into it too. The only little problem in creating this file using *ed* is to find a way of entering the line with only '.' on it: this exercise is left for you to consider. There are several solutions.

mail can also be used where UNIX systems are networked together; this is a particularly powerful means of interchanging files, but is a topic that is beyond the scope of this text. It does however demonstrate something of the usefulness of the *mail* program.

11.4 A management philosophy

From its origins, the philosophy of UNIX has been very much associated with the concept of a community of cooperating users. There is some protection afforded for the critical parts of the operating system, to prevent any change by unauthorised users (hence the need for a super-user); but there is no strong hierarchy of protection levels, and beyond providing this basic degree of self-defence, UNIX provides relatively little to restrict a user's actions.

The software tools that are provided for system management are all generally concerned with retrospective applications of this, preferring to audit the use of filestore and cpu time rather than to restrict it during use. (As examples of such utility programs, *df* gives the amount of free space left on a disc, *du* tells us the amount of filestore used by the current directory and its subdirectories, and *ac* monitors the amount of access time used—although this needs to be specifically enabled to do so.)

Beyond allocating users to membership of groups (in the UNIX sense), and setting up default forms of file access, there is relatively little that a project manager can do in order to exercise immediate and interactive control over his team, although the previous sections suggest various means for keeping abreast of developments. For any full control of software development, a system such as SCCS is needed in addition to the UNIX V7 facilities; and this has been included in the UNIX System V that has been developed from UNIX V7. In summary, team management is rather constrained on UNIX V7.

11.5   Protecting your investments

Software is produced by very labour-intensive means, and so every prudent manager or research team leader likes to be able to make backup copies of the contents of filestore on a regular basis, as a form of insurance against accidents—whatever the form. The very large capacity of modern disc systems especially means that so many of our 'eggs' will be in the same magnetic basket!

The fastest and easiest form of making backup copies, where a second disc drive is available, is to make a disc-to-disc copy using the *dump* utility. The backup disc can then just be a direct copy of the image of the main disc.

A cheaper medium for longer-term archiving, or bulk copying, is digital magnetic tape. The *dump* utility will provide an incremental dump of files on to tape, and can even be set to dump only those files that have been modified since a particular date, i.e. the date of the last dump. Since *dump* keeps a record of the times and dates of dumps in its own database file, a continuous scheme for making backup copies is fairly easy to devise. The *dumpdir* program will provide a directory listing of the contents of a tape.

Merely storing our files on tape is not enough in itself, since to be of use we have to be able to copy them back too. The utility program *restor* reverses the actions of *dump* and can be used to retrieve anything, ranging from one file to the contents of a whole disc.

There is also the *tar* (tape archiver) program which can be used to copy individual files to tapes and to retrieve them—and which provides a sufficiently straightforward interface to the tape system for most requirements.

The reader will probably by now have concluded that UNIX is an operating system built for users rather than for managers. This is very true, and is one of its great strengths. UNIX provides a basic operating system with powerful facilities for building one's own software tools, which can be for management too of course. Management needs to be superimposed on programming as needed, rather than carried as a continual overhead and encumbrance. However, it should be noted that this is one area where the re-worked forms of UNIX and the UNIX System V implementation have provided additional features to support the needs of the commercial user, for whom management of the work is much more of a priority than it is in academic circles.

12

A few more software tools

12.1 Introduction

The underlying theme so far has been to describe the software tools that are available on the UNIX system in terms of their potential for problem-solving, as well as to indicate where facilities exist, and can appropriately be used, for the construction of new software tools in support of a problem. This chapter sums up some of the points involved and concludes Part II by introducing some rather specialist forms of software tool that UNIX has to offer.

12.2 When to write programs

The UNIX facilities for conventional programming and shell programming were introduced in Chapters 6 and 7, with particular emphasis being placed upon the ways in which these could be integrated. One example of this is the use of pro-forma programs, giving an individually tailored means of generating quite powerful facilities from a number of simple but powerful modules: some written as shell programs, and some as conventional programs in C. In particular, considerable use has been made of the facility for redirecting the standard output of processes, since for many tasks this can considerably simplify the form of the program required.

Shell programming can become addictive, and an addict will usually be characterised by his strong desire to tackle every problem by using the *shell*, so defying the principles of good engineering practice, whereby we try to use the tools best suited to solving a particular task.

The balance between the proportion of programs constructed using the *shell*, and that constructed in more conventional programming languages, is something that changes with growing expertise and with the nature of the current problem being tackled. We can pursue the engineering analogy a little further; in the ideal we would draw out the various programs and subprograms needed to construct our application program from our standard stock, and 'bolt' them together with pipes and *shell* constructs. Pragmatism suggests though that we might well have to hand-craft some of the units needed using conventional programming methods, since we are writing programs, not building girder bridges.

Sometimes the choice of language to use is obvious: number-crunching problems need a language such as FORTRAN; problems needing complex record-structures will be easier to handle with a language such as Pascal or Modula-2; and file handling exercises may be best performed in COBOL. Other choices may be less easily resolved; text handling in particular is not very good in many of the more popular languages, and is of mixed convenience in the *shell*. Some criteria may be needed to help us in making the choice, and the following three are suggested as possible starters.

(1) Determine a level of complexity that is to be regarded as the working maximum when using the *shell*, e.g. no more than three levels of indentation.

(2)   Examine any large conventionally programmed programs to see if they could be reduced to a series of smaller programs, and whether some of these might then be sufficiently general purpose to be used on other problems. There is no point in repeatedly writing the same software—it just gives more opportunity to make new mistakes.

(3)   Consider whether any existing programs could be restructured to use the standard input and standard output only; and if so, whether this would make them more general purpose and re-usable.

While our programming practices should not be bound by unduly rigid guidelines, some orderly analysis of our methods or designs is rarely wasted effort.

In making the choice it is also relevant to note that there are many UNIX utility programs that can be used to provide 'system' information, *test, du, df, ls, who*, etc. There is also a good range that can be used for handling character strings and performing pattern matching tasks, e.g. *grep, diff, awk, ed.* These provide useful programming tools for those tasks for which many conventional programming languages are less well provided. Similarly, database exercises may also be well suited to shell programming, since they are mainly concerned with handling characters and matching patterns.

Choosing the software tool for a task is very much a case of 'horses for courses'—and we need to determine whether our problem needs a plough horse or a thoroughbred!

12.3   Building software tools

While Part I generally concentrates upon how to use the software tools that are provided as part of the UNIX system, Part II is much more concerned with how these can be used to build further problem-specific software tools as an aid to problem-solving. The term 'software tool' has been used very frequently, and perhaps should be more fully clarified for this section. By a 'software tool', we mean a program that is used primarily as an aid to constructing programs, e.g. a text editor, compiler, or directory listing utility, rather than one which is directly involved in the final application.

UNIX is generally regarded as providing a very good tool-building environment, and this section looks at the techniques associated with the use of such tool-building tools.

We may have a number of reasons for producing software tools of our own—perhaps to improve an existing facility or to provide an extension to one, to improve the user's interface to a complex program, to assist us in controlling or documenting a project, to help with the housekeeping of our files—the list is virtually endless, and the emphasis will change according to our problem and our environment.

We have already seen some examples of how the powerful forms of shell programming can be used to create some of these facilities, in the examples of the last few chapters. These were concerned with tools required to assist with a particular problem, or a particular facet of a problem, whereas this section is concerned more with how the tools themselves might be structured. Two examples are provided—a 'help' facility and an interactive utility format.

12.3.1   A 'help' utility

Many operating systems provide some form of 'help' facility by which, on typing the command *help*, the user will be reminded of how to enter commands, by providing information to help him select the command needed and the options that might be suitable for the particular problem. On some systems, this utility will even assist in the creation of the necessary command lines, using a step-by-step dialogue with the user.

For the UNIX system, the nearest equivalent to a 'help' facility is the *man* utility, which copies a section of the UNIX manual describing the appropriate utility program to our screen. *man* is a useful aid for the more experienced UNIX user, but for the beginner there are two problems encountered in making use of it. These are as follows:

(i) we need to know which section of the manual contains the information required in the appropriate level of detail;

(ii) we need to know which utility program is the appropriate one for the task that is to be performed.

The first problem is really not too severe, since in the beginning we are almost always concerned with the information contained in Section 1 of the UNIX manual, covering the use of the utility programs themselves. The second is much more awkward, especially given the UNIX affinity for the use of fairly cryptic and terse program names, e.g. *grep, cat, ls*. Figure 12.1 suggests a shell program to provide a simple 'help' facility on UNIX,

```
case $# in
     0) echo "To get a list of common UNIX commands, type:-"
        echo "       help commands  "
        echo
        echo
        echo "To get information on any individual command, type:-"
        echo "       help <command_name> "
        echo
        echo ;;
     1) if test $1 = commands
        then cat /etc/avcomms
        else man 1 $1
        fi;;
     *) echo "Too many parameters"
esac
```

Fig. 12.1 A shell program to provide a simple help facility

and which can be installed in /usr/bin so that it can be used by all users on the system. It is by no means all-encompassing, but does provide a rather more easily remembered interface for the user who just wants some information about using a utility. The user simply types

```
$ help
```

to obtain the messages

```
        To get a list of common UNIX commands, type:-
             help commands


        To get information on any individual command, type:-
             help <command_name>
```

Table 12.1   Commonly used UNIX commands

adb	du	mesg	sort
as	echo	mkdir	spell
at	em	mv	split
awk	f77	newgrp	strip
basename	factor	passwd	stty
bc	file	pc	su
cal	find	pr	tail
calendar	grep	prolog	tbl
cat	help	ps	test
cb	kill	pubindex	time
cc	ld	pwd	touch
cd	lint	qstate	tr
chmod	ln	ratfor	troff
chown	login	refer	true
cmp	logout	rev	tty
comm	lp	rm	uniq
cp	ls	roff	units
cptree	m2c	scrpr	wait
crypt	m4	sed	wc
date	mail	sh	who
dc	make	size	write
diff	man	sleep	yacc

By typing the command

```
$ help   commands
```

he can then obtain the list given in Table 12.1 (from the file /etc/avcomms).

Table 12.1 lists only the names of the available utility programs, but it is fairly easy to change the format of the output simply by modifying the file /etc/avcomms to the required format. This will then provide more information as appropriate. To obtain the entry for a particular utility program we then enter (say):

```
$ help ls
```

as a rather more memorable line than

```
$ man 1 ls
```

12.3.2   An interactive utility interface

While the previous example suggested a way to improve our interface to a particular utility, just by wrapping a shell program around it to improve the presentation, this is not always the most effective form to use. For example, some of the entries in the UNIX manual are not particularly easy to follow, given the rather terse style in use; and when dealing with a utility that is used infrequently, interpreting the information given in the manual can prove a rather time-consuming exercise. A method of improving upon this is to write an interactive shell program which constructs the parameters via a dialogue with the user. The example used here is *chmod*, for which a very simplified but rigid form of 'user interface' was suggested in the example of 'meonly' in Chapter 11.

To handle dialogue in a shell program, the *shell* provides two useful facilities: the *echo* utility, which causes the program to write messages to the user; and the *read* function, which places the words of a line of text typed in on the standard input into a set of shell variables given as the arguments of the call. If only one shell variable is given, then the whole line is placed in that one variable.

Figure 12.2 suggests a way of modifying *chmod* using these facilities. So that we can keep the same name when using our modified form, we can place our own version of 'chmod' in one of our own directories (say 'bin'), and then modify the '.profile' file so that the search path for the *shell* is changed to always search this directory first when seeking an executable file. This can be done by inserting the line

```
PATH=:/..../NewUser/bin:/bin:/usr/bin
```

where the ':' character separates the directories that comprise the current 'search path' as defined by the shell variable PATH. Note that the full specification of the pathname to NewUser/bin must be provided, so that we can use the programs within it regardless of which directory is our current directory.

When this is done, we can then type the command

```
$ chmod
```

or

```
$ chmod <filename>
```

and our own version of 'chmod' will be used as a buffer between ourselves and the standard UNIX version stored in /bin. The new version then prompts us for a yes/no answer for granting each form of access permission to the user, group and world classes of system user, prefixing each request in turn with a suitable prompt, such as:

```
u_:
```

or

```
w_:
```

for the 'user' or 'world' classes respectively. From our responses it then assembles the appropriate command strings for *chmod*, and modifies the access permission for the file accordingly. So the first part of our dialogue will look like this:

```
$ chmod subs.f
enter y for each form of access granted
to user, group and others in turn
read access
u_:y
write access
u_:y
execute access
u_:n
read access
g_:y
write access
g_:n
< and so on >
```

```
: an interactive form for the chmod utility
: stored in NewUser/bin/chmod
:
: check first for a filename as parameter, if none
: supplied then prompt for one
:
if test $# -eq 0
then
     echo -n "filename_:"
     read file
else
     file=$1
fi
:
: remove all access permission from file
:
/bin/chmod a-rwx $file
:
: now set access permission for the three classes of user
:
echo "enter y for each form of access granted"
echo "to user, group and others in turn"
:
for i in u g o
do
     mode=''
     echo "read access"
     echo -n $i"_:"
     read answer
     if test $answer = 'y'
     then
          mode=r
     fi
     echo "write access"
     echo -n $i"_:"
     read answer
     if test $answer = 'y'
     then
          mode=w$mode
     fi
     echo "execute access"
     echo -n $i"_:"
     read answer
     if test $answer = 'y'
     then
          mode=x$mode
     fi
     /bin/chmod $i"+"$mode $file
done
:
: now display final form of access permitted
:
ls -l $file
```

Fig. 12.2 An example of an interactive form for *chmod*

This initial dialogue will direct *chmod* to set our own access permission for 'subs.f' to read and write access, and to grant read access but not write access permission for other members of our group. The remaining prompts take the same form.

Several infrequently used programs lend themselves to this treatment; even *help* might benefit. However, it should be noted that the technique soon becomes rather tedious if used frequently and so should be saved for those occasions where it can save us the time needed to re-familiarise ourselves with the use of some program which has a fairly complex set of options (examples of such include possibly *dd, dump* and *tar*).

12.4   Some tool-building utility programs

This section briefly surveys some of the specialist utility programs that are provided on UNIX for the construction of other programs. The names of some of the utility programs would seem to be even more influenced by Tolkein's *Hobbit* than usual—*awk, lex,* and *yacc,* all have a rather forbidding note to them. This is an appropriate warning to the would-be user, since they are not the most simple programs to use.

The rest of this section gives a short introduction to the utilities that are likely to be explored at some point, although no attempt is made to do more than indicate the facilities provided and to give a short example of their use.

12.4.1   *dc*—the desk calculator

dc provides an interpretive desk calculator language capable of working to different number bases and varying degrees of precision. The latter feature does not of course transcend the normal limitation imposed by the quality of one's data—garbage in, garbage out still applies.

The format used by *dc* is reverse polish, and it can be used directly or via simple programs which combine its statements. The following very trivial example consists of a program which takes a given decimal number input by the user, and multiplies it by the constant 0.6 before printing the result on the standard output. While trivial, it is a useful means for making a number of simple calculations in the absence of a pocket calculator.

```
0.6
?
*pq
```

To make any real use of this we probably need to place it in a file (say 'xscale') and use it within a shell program such as the following:

```
while test xscale
do
     dc xscale
done
```

In this case we have used an infinite loop (not very elegant) and the user terminates the loop by pressing control-C to abort the shell program.

For more ambitious applications, the C-type language *bc* can be used as a pre-processor for *dc* in order to provide a 'better' interface (depending upon one's views on the subject of C).

12.4.2   *awk*—a pattern matching language

The pattern matching utility program *grep* was introduced earlier as a program that can be invaluable when performing particular problem-oriented tasks. Its ability to scan files of text in order to match character patterns makes it a particularly useful interactive tool, but it is less suited to use with shell programming techniques and so UNIX provides the *awk* language as a more powerful and programmable pattern matching facility.

awk (whose name is derived from the initials of its creators), is a pattern scanning and processing language. The syntax is remarkably terse, even by the Trappist standards of UNIX, offering both a challenge and a barrier to the would-be user. *awk* supports a programming 'language', and there are two formats for using this. In the first format, the program is given as a part of the actual *shell* command and, as discussed later, this can be useful in allowing the *shell* to substitute for metacharacters. In the second format, the program is stored in a program file that is read by *awk*. A useful extension to use in naming such a file is '.awk', although this is not a default and is purely a convention which aids housekeeping.

The following example shows both forms of use. We take a data file made up from a series of entries, each of which consists of a single line **record** that is stored in a standard format. Each record is in turn divided up into a number of **fields**, and the fields are separated by tab characters. This gives *awk* a means of identifying the limits of each field of a record, while still allowing the use of space characters to give legibility. The problem is assumed to be that of some simple record keeping for a small company, so that various figures and data can be easily extracted by various programs; perhaps for the construction of a monthly report, or for a more immediate use.

```
Rusty Bolts Co   Falkirk 10000 5
Scrap Metals Inc     Stirling 50000 10
Old Iron Ltd     Falkirk 23000 4
Pressed Metals   Falkirk 40000 10
Falkirk Iron Co Stirling 10000 1
Ferroco Stirling     21000 4
```

Fig. 12.3   A simple data file, where fields are separated by tab characters

Note: the fields represent the following:
 (i)   the name of a company;
 (ii) the base town of that company;
 (iii) the value of transactions performed with that company;
 (iv) the number of transactions performed with that company.

An example data file of this type is given in Fig. 12.3, and consists of a simple series of records. Each contains the name of a company, the town where its premises are situated, the value of business conducted with the company in the previous year, and the number of orders involved (the construction of such a file clearly offers good scope for the use of a pro-forma program). Our program performs the following sequence of actions:

 (i)   extract all of the records for companies in a given town;
 (ii)   sort these records into alphabetical order by company name;
 (iii) print out the records, together with the total business value conducted with the companies in that town, and the number of transactions that were involved.

Shell programming methods are appropriate for this program, as the sequence involved is well-defined and suited to the use of pipes to link the component processes. *awk* can be used for the first and last tasks, while the *sort* utility is of course ideal for the second task. As is usually the case with shell programs, we can develop the program in a stepwise manner, testing at each stage.

We begin with step (i). The name of the town in which the company's premises are situated is stored as the second field of a record, so we first need to extract each record in which the second field matches the chosen string. The shell command

```
$ awk "BEGIN{ FS="\t"} /Falkirk/"  datafile
```

will print out all lines from file 'datafile' which contain the string 'Falkirk'; the '/' characters define the match pattern to use. So using the file of Fig. 12.3, our output from this would be:

```
Rusty Bolts Co  Falkirk 10000 5
Old Iron Ltd    Falkirk 23000 4
Pressed Metals  Falkirk 40000 10
Falkirk Iron Co Stirling 10000 1
```

To explain this a little more, an *awk* program is made up from a set of pattern matches and actions, the latter contained within the braces '{ }'. By preceding an action with the 'BEGIN' statement, as in:

```
BEGIN {FS="\t"}
```

we direct *awk* that this particular action should be performed only once at the beginning of the program, rather than for every line that matches the preceding pattern. (There is also an 'END' directive to be used in the same way.) So our *awk* 'program' is now:

```
BEGIN {FS="\t"} /Falkirk/
```

This declares the **field separator** to be the tab character ('FS' is a standard variable within *awk*), then extracts all lines that contain a match to the given pattern of 'Falkirk', and writes them to the standard output. There is an element of 'forward look' here, in that we have not yet needed to use the field separator.

As the next step in developing this first part of our program, we wish to restrict the pattern matching to only those records where the string 'Falkirk' appears in the second field of the record. To do this, we preceded the match pattern by '$2~', to indicate that the pattern matching command is to apply only to the second field of a record. So our program now becomes:

```
$ awk 'BEGIN{ FS="\t"} $2 ~ /Falkirk/' datafile
```

and this produces as its output:

```
Rusty Bolts Co  Falkirk 10000 5
Old Iron Ltd    Falkirk 23000 4
Pressed Metals  Falkirk 40000 10
```

Note that we now need to place the 'program' between single quotes. This is to ensure that the *shell* will not attempt to treat the $2 as a shell parameter. (Remember that with double quote marks, some metacharacters, including $, are not quoted. By using single quotes we ensure that the $ character will be quoted, and hence passed on to *awk*.)

To make this program more general, and easier to use, we can place it in the file 'extract', and use it as a shell program. However, this complicates the setting up of the pattern to be used as a match, assuming that we are interested in other places than Falkirk alone. This would require the use of shell parameters, and these in turn must *not* be quoted, so that the *shell* can make the appropriate substitutions before passing the string to *awk*! So the equivalent one line shell program now becomes

```
awk 'BEGIN{ FS="\t"} $2 ~ /'$1'/' $2
```

Here the first instance of $2 is within the single quotes and hence quoted, so it is passed on to *awk* unchanged; however, $1 is unquoted (the quoting terminates before it, and begins again afterwards), so that the *shell* will substitute the string of characters making up the first parameter of the process call in its place. The second instance of $2 is also unquoted and the *shell* substitutes the appropriate filename in its place.

We can now use this program in the form

```
$ extract Falkirk datafile
```

to obtain the same result as before, but now using a more generalised program.

The second sequential task of our program is very simple, since we can sort the records using the standard *sort* utility. As the name of the company is the first field of each record, we simply direct *sort* to use the first characters as its sorting key; the 'extract' program then takes the form:

```
awk 'BEGIN{FS="\t"} $2 ~ /'$1'/' $2 | sort
```

Here the output from *awk* is piped into *sort* to produce the following output:

```
Old Iron Ltd    Falkirk 23000 4
Pressed Metals  Falkirk 40000 10
Rusty Bolts Co  Falkirk 10000 5
```

For the third task, we now need to write an *awk* program which will sum the values of the transactions and sum the number of transactions involved. A program to do this,

```
BEGIN { FS="\t"
    total = 0
    value = 0 }
{ print }
{value = value + $3}
{total = total + $4}
END{ printf "Total no of transactions " total "\n"
     printf "Total value of transactions " value "\n" }
```

Fig. 12.4 The *awk* program 'extract.awk'

'extract.awk', is given in Fig. 12.4. We can now extend our program 'extract' to pipe the output of *sort* into this, so that it takes its final form of:

```
awk 'BEGIN{FS="\t"} $2 ~ /'$1'/' $2 | sort | awk -f extract.awk
```

Here the '-f' flag directs *awk* to take its program from the file whose name follows the option flag. So if we now give the command:

```
BEGIN { FS = "\t" ; OFS = "\t" ; totnormal = 0 ; totovert = 0 ;
        print "Number", "Emp.name", "Basic", "O'time", "Basic", "O'time", "Total";
        print "        ", "      ", "Hours", "Hours", "Pay", "Pay", "Pay"}
{if ($3 == "ill")
        print $1,$2,0,0,0,0,0
 else {
        npay = $3*10;
        opay = $4*12.5;
        tpay = npay+opay;
        totnormal += npay;
        totovert += opay;
        print $1,$2,$3,$4,"$"npay,"$"opay,"$"tpay
      }
}
END { print "Cumulative", "Totals", "-", "-", "$"totnormal, "$"totovert,
      "$"totnormal+totovert}
```

Fig. 12.5 The *awk* program 'calcpay.awk' for a spreadsheet calculation

```
$ extract Falkirk datafile
```

then the final output from this looks like:

```
Old Iron Ltd    Falkirk 23000 4
Pressed Metals  Falkirk 40000 10
Rusty Bolts Co  Falkirk 10000 5
Total no of transactions 19
Total value of transactions 73000
```

In this example, the program 'extract.awk' takes the simple form of a series of actions, since the pattern matching has been separated out in order to be able to parameterise it via the *shell*. Actions for which no pattern is specified are performed on every line of the file, and hence for each line of the input the line is printed out, and the value of and number of transactions are added to their respective totals. Note too that *awk* provides a number of built-in functions such as 'printf'.

From the example, it can be seen that *awk* can be particularly useful for handling and processing small databases. The combination of its use with the powers available from shell programming greatly extends its scope, and allows the possibility of constructing various analysis and presentation tools with relative ease—once the initial mastery of the *awk* format has been achieved!

As a further example of the use of *awk*, the production of **spreadsheet** output represents only a fairly small step on from the previous example. The *awk* program 'calcpay.awk', shown in Fig. 12.5, will perform a simple pay-roll calculation using a data file such as the file 'paydata' shown in Fig. 12.6. This contains the employee number,

```
12345   Smith,JM      37      0
22456   Jones,SP      37      0
76983   Jackson,P     37      6
77233   Jones,LL      i11
45443   Collins,PC    37      4
12294   Davies,PP     30      0
44331   Harrison,J    37      3
```

Fig. 12.6   A sample data file 'paydata' for the spreadsheet calculation

name, hours worked and overtime worked for each employee that week. (Note the use of the assignment 'x + =' in calcpay.awk, as shorthand for 'x = x +', a typical C language format!) Then the command

```
$ awk -f calcpay.awk paydata
```

will produce the print-out shown in Fig. 12.7.

If preferred, we can also use *sort* with this to re-order the contents of 'paydata' before processing them, should we prefer to have our print-out ordered by, say, name of employee, record number, or hours of overtime worked.

Number	Emp.name	Basic Hours	O'time Hours	Basic Pay	O'time Pay	Total Pay
12345	Smith,JM	37	0	$370	$0	$370
22456	Jones,SP	37	0	$370	$0	$370
76983	Jackson,P	37	6	$370	$75	$445
77233	Jones,LL	0	0	0	0	0
45443	Collins,PC	37	4	$370	$50	$420
12294	Davies,PP	30	0	$300	$0	$300
44331	Harrison,J	37	3	$370	$37.5	$407.5
Cumulative	Totals	-	-	$2150	$162.5	$2312.5

Fig. 12.7

12.4.3 *lex*—a lexical analyser

lex is a program which can be used to generate source files for programs which require a simple lexical analysis of text files. Its output takes the form of a source file which can be directly routed to the C compiler *cc*. It is really intended for use in combination with a utility program such as *yacc* (yet another compiler compiler) to assist in the writing of compilers, or similar text processing exercises, by dealing with some of the more mechanical tasks involved. It is mentioned here merely as an example of the variety of utility programs that UNIX provides.

This is a good point at which to end Part II of this text. Part I introduced the UNIX philosophy, which was that of providing an operating system which could be used as a base on which a user could create his own software tools and develop his application programs. Part II has tried to show how the UNIX system can most effectively be used to meet a user's application requirements.

Chapter 12 provides rather a superficial level of cover, because it is intended to demonstrate how a user can proceed past the first basic level of familiarisation with UNIX, and to indicate the facilities which then become available to him. The UNIX system is far too large for a comprehensive coverage to be within the scope of a text such as this.

Part III

Since this text set out with the principal aim of trying to show a new (or prospective) user of a UNIX system how its facilities might be effectively used to tackle their particular problems, there may seem to be relatively little rationale for including the topics of this third section of the book, which deals, at least in outline, with the behind-the-scenes aspects of UNIX. The justification is that there are inevitably those problems for which a solution may require a more detached understanding of the mechanics of the system. A particular example of such a problem is the need to use a peripheral device that is not normally supported by the UNIX operating system. The would-be device user is faced with the questions of how difficult it is to write a device driver program to integrate the device with the UNIX system, and how much detailed knowledge of the UNIX system will be needed to support this task.

Neither question will by any means be completely answered by the topics and features described in Part III, but having some idea of how UNIX and its filestore are organised should help when making plans for those solutions that need such facilities. This section of the text aims to help such planning by providing an overview of the workings of the UNIX system, so that by a top-down progression, the reader can be guided to the appropriate headings of the UNIX manual in which to find the detailed information needed. Note that most of the topics involved refer to items that appear in Sections 4 and 5 of the UNIX manual. In this sense Part III points to the relevant reference material for the topics covered, rather than providing any in-depth levels of detail.

There is one other justification. If by now the reader has really begun to grapple with the use of UNIX, then perhaps a little curiosity about how some of the facilities are provided is not to be discouraged!

13

More about files—and a bit about devices too

13.1   Introduction

The first part of the following text provides a reminder about the features of the file system that have been emphasised previously.

One of the key features in the design of the UNIX filestore is that files themselves have no structure, in the sense that they are not internally organised in any way by the file handling routines. Any structure that a file possesses is imposed by the programs that create and use it, not by the system itself. Each file is viewed by the file handling system as simply being a sequence of eight-bit bytes. As an example of this, were we to examine a file that had been created by the text editor *ed*, then we would find that it was stored as a sequence of lines of characters, each line being terminated by the 'newline' character. For example, the line

        A line.

would be stored as a sequence of eight bytes, with successive bytes containing the ASCII codes for the characters 'A', 'space', 'l', 'i', 'n', 'e', '.', 'newline' as follows. Here the codes are given in octal (base 8):

        101, 040, 154, 151, 156, 145, 056, 012

and the next byte in the file will then contain the first character of the next line.

13.1.1   Examining files—the *od* utility program

On some occasions we may wish to examine our files using a form such as that used in the above example, printing out a suitable representation of the bit pattern contained in each byte or word. Such a facility is useful for examining files that contain various forms of data: character, integer, mixed types, etc. On UNIX the appropriate program for this task is the *od* utility, which will print out all or part of a file using one of a number of output formats; sometimes it may be useful to print out the file several times in different formats.

The output format for *od* is determined using the normal method of selection of options. The options are as follows.

-b   interpret each byte as an octal value.
-c   interpret each byte as an ASCII character. Where the character is a non-printing character, it will be printed using the same format as for '-b', or using the C language format if it is a formatting character; e.g. newline becomes '\n'.
-d   interprets each word (two bytes) as a decimal value.
-o   interprets each word as an octal value (the default option).
-x   interprets each word as a hexadecimal value.

od (rather confusingly the name stands for 'octal dump', despite the other options), will print out the value of eight bytes on each line of the standard output, and will precede each line with the address within the file of that particular line—i.e. the address of the first byte. Empty lines, where all characters are nulls, are not printed.

The following three lines are examples of the output of *od*, taking a C source program as the input file and using the '–b' option:

```
0000000 043 151 156 143 154 165 144 145 040 074 163 164 144 151 157 056
0000020 150 076 012 012 145 170 164 145 162 156 040 163 165 142 061 050
0000040 051 073 012 057 052 011 163 141 155 160 154 145 040 103 040 160
```

od is a useful debugging aid in its own right, as well as providing a means for checking the structures within files when necessary. This is particularly true for a problem such as that discussed in Chapter 9, where a program may have been obtained from another (non-UNIX) system. *od* can then be used to examine the structure of the file itself (e.g. does it pad all lines out to a standard length with space characters or nulls, etc.) and, at a later stage, of the data that it may produce once running.

13.2   i-nodes and their use

In introducing the filestore in Chapter 4, some mention was made of the i-nodes, and of the way in which a directory file only contains a little of the information about a file—more precisely, only the name and 'i-number' of the file. (To check this, try using *od* on one of your directories.) We can find the values of the i-numbers of our files by using the '-i' option with *ls*, as in

```
$ ls -i
```

which might produce something of the form:

```
1187  main.f
1476  subs.f
```

This indicates that 'main.f' has i-number value 1187, etc. Similarly, for full details on a file we can use '-li', as in

```
$ ls -li
```

which for the previous example might give:

```
1187 -rw-rw-r--  1  NewUser    2315   March  6  10:47  main.f
1476 -rw-rw-r--  1  NewUser    4241   March 10  14:32  subs.f
```

13.2.1   i-numbers, i-nodes and the i-table

To find out more about a file, or to access it in any way, the file handling procedures must make use of the i-number obtained from the directory. The purpose of the i-number is to act as an index for the position of the appropriate i-node for the file within a large table of i-nodes, the **i-table**. The i-table too is stored in the filestore, since it must reside on the same device as the files and directories to which it refers.

In practice, the lowest numbered block on a disc is known as the **superblock**. This contains assorted information about the filestore and the disc itself, and one of these items of information is the storage location of the i-table on the disc: it is usually stored in the blocks immediately following the superblock. So, given the i-number of a file, the file handling procedures can use this as an index value for the file's entry in the i-table; this is the i-node which acts as the file header for the file. This also explains why a file can be referenced by more than one entry in a directory, as well as under different names—the different entries simply contain the same i-number.

13.2.2 Inside the i-node

The i-node for a file is the main repository for information about that file, since the directory (or directories) only contain the filename and i-number, and the file buffer holds only the data contained within the file. All other information about a file, such as the access protection codes, the owner's user identity and group identity, the size of the file, etc., is contained within the i-node. On UNIX V7 an i-node occupies 64 bytes of a disc block, and hence each 512 byte block of the disc will hold eight i-nodes (or eight entries in the i-table if one prefers to view it that way). A full description of the internal structure of an i-node can be obtained from Section 5 of the UNIX documentation (under the heading of *filsys*).

The last 40 bytes of the i-node contain the addresses of 13 blocks on the disc, each address requiring three bytes and one spare at the end. The first ten addresses are used to hold the addresses of the first ten blocks of the file buffer itself. Should the file be longer than 5120 bytes (ten blocks), it will require additional blocks for the buffer and so the next block address in the i-node (11) contains the address of a disc block which in turn contains the addresses of the next 128 blocks of the file (i.e. a form of indirect addressing).

This still restricts the possible size of a file, even if the limit is now much higher; so for a file that requires more than 138 blocks, the next block address entry in the i-node (12) is used to contain the address of a block which in turn holds the addresses of 128 blocks, each of which contains the addresses of a further 128 blocks of the buffer (double indirection). The very largest files can exceed even the high limits provided by this scheme and will need the services of the thirteenth entry in the i-node. This provides a triple indirection scheme of block addressing that should suffice for almost any file that can be held on the filestore.

Figure 13.1 shows how the i-node is used to link the actual disc blocks used for the file buffer for the first 138 blocks of a file, i.e. up to the first level of indirection as described above.

It might seem from this description that the use of large files might slow the execution of a process, since accesses to the higher numbered blocks of the buffer will require increasing numbers of disc accesses to obtain their physical locations. In practice this is not noticeably so, partly because the disc handling system of UNIX uses a buffer space in memory to hold copies of blocks, and organises this in rather the manner of a **cache**, operating a 'read-ahead' scheme of pre-fetching disc blocks to anticipate some of the disc accesses that will be needed.

To give a very simple example of how the addressing scheme works, if we want to obtain byte number 6170 of a file, then we begin by dividing its position by 512 to work out that it must lie within the thirteenth block of the file buffer. Using the i-number for the file, we then obtain the address of the block containing the i-node and read that. Since the number of the block we want is greater than 10, we obtain from the i-node the

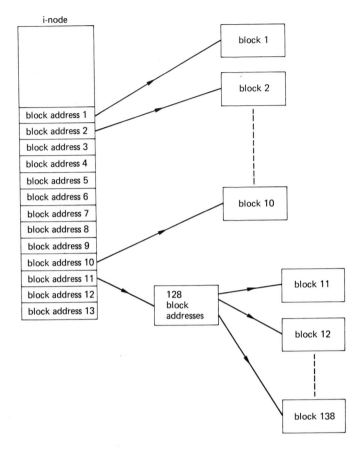

Fig. 13.1   Accessing the blocks of the file buffer from the i-node; the first two levels

eleventh block address and proceed to read that block. The third disc address stored in this block is then the address of the thirteenth block of the file buffer, and this too is read in turn so that we can extract the appropriate byte.

However, in practice such an individual access would be unusual, since most processes read through a file sequentially, so allowing the look-ahead mechanism to function very effectively.

13.3   Devices on UNIX

It is a part of the UNIX philosophy that devices and files are treated in identical fashion by user software, so permitting such useful facilities as the redirection of standard input and standard output. The protocols used for accessing and using a file are identical with those for accessing and using the device driver process that acts as the system's interface to a particular physical device such as a printer, a terminal or a plotter.

13.3.1   Devices as special files

For each device used on the system, there is an associated **special file** within the directory

```
/dev
```

and any accesses to such files, using the normal protocols, will cause the appropriate device driver process to be activated. It is this facility that allows such utility programs as *write* to function so easily. We can copy a file to a device, such as a terminal (say 'ttyp'), rather as we copy one file to another. We might use a command such as

```
$ cat myfile.f >/dev/ttyp
```

or

```
$ cp myfile.f /dev/ttyp
```

and either of these will result in the contents of 'myfile.f' appearing on the screen of terminal 'ttyp'. Of course, structured devices such as discs are duly protected against such arbitrary access!

13.3.2   Mountable devices

Where the filestore is spread over more than one disc pack, then those discs other than the system disc holding the root directory will be mountable, and hence inherently removable.

To use the filestore segment maintained on a mountable device we must first link it into the filestore hierarchy by using the *mount* utility. This normally takes a form such as

```
$ /etc/mount /dev/rm03 /mnt
```

The first parameter of this, '/dev/rm03', is used to specify the physical or logical device itself (in this case drive 'rm03'), while the second parameter, '/mnt', specifies which directory in the system filestore will be used to provide the link to the extra filestore of this device.

The procedure for dismounting a device is very similar, and for the above example the reverse action is performed via

```
$ /etc/umount /dev/rm03
```

which requires only the device to be identified.

13.4   i-nodes for special files

Since a device is accessed as a special file, it is reasonable to expect that its i-node will be different from the i-nodes of normal files in some way. In fact many of the fields of the i-node are used in much the same way as for a normal file, but of course the table of 13 disc block addresses is no longer relevant. For a special file, the i-node contains instead a pair of numbers in place of the first disc block address, and these specify the actual device type (i.e. which device driver process should be activated), and if appropriate, the sub-device number. The sub-device number is used for those devices where one controller may interface to several devices, such as a terminal multiplexer or a disc controller.

When the file handling procedures wish to access a special file, the initial steps of accessing the i-node are performed just as for any other file, and it is only when the i-node is used that the information must be interpreted in an appropriate manner.

One last point about devices is that UNIX recognises two classes of devices, **block** and **character**. Block devices are devices such as discs, which normally require some form of memory buffer space on the system, while character devices are all other devices that are not block devices. (The term 'character' is not wholly accurate, since the characters might represent all sorts of data forms besides ASCII characters.) When being used in a non-standard form, even discs and tapes can sometimes be handled as character devices.

One of the great benefits of the UNIX filestore organisation is that it allows this unified treatment of files and devices—and as the preceding sections show, this makes for a very elegant and effective programming environment.

14
Processes on UNIX

14.1 Introduction

It is prudent to begin by providing a reminder of what is meant by the term 'process' within the context of this chapter.

A user's files contain **programs**, i.e. sequences of instructions. These may be human-readable **source** programs, i.e. the original ASCII text of the program as written by the programmer; **object** programs, consisting of the machine instruction codes generated by a translator such as a compiler, but not yet linked to any support library routines; and machine-readable **executable** programs, usually machine instructions that can be copied directly into the main memory of the computer and executed by the central processor unit. The last class also includes **shell programs**, which are interpreted by the *shell*.

When an executable program is executed by the processor, either directly or via the *shell* acting as an interpreter, it becomes known as a **process**. The act of executing a process can be considered as the task of advancing it step-by-step from one state to another, where the **state** of a process is represented by the current contents of the cpu registers and the contents of the data storage areas that the process possesses in main memory. A process is executed under the control of the operating system, which handles such tasks as determining when the process is to be scheduled to **run**, and if necessary organising for it to be temporarily copied out to backing store (swapped) should the pressure for memory space require this. These actions of the operating system are designed so as to be carried out in a form that is invisible to the process itself—and by preserving the state of a process at any time when it becomes suspended, so that it can be resumed unchanged, repeated runs of the same process with the same input data will always generate the same results, regardless of how the scheduling is varied.

Processes may themselves communicate with the operating system in order to request information (e.g. time of day, open a file, etc.), or to request actions that may affect their own execution or involve the operating system in executing other processes. It is the facilities that are provided by UNIX under these headings (often known as **system services**) that form the principal subject matter of this chapter.

14.2 Running multiple processes—synchronisation of processes

So far in this book, and particularly in the examples, it has generally been assumed that a user will only wish to run one process at a time from his terminal. After starting a process, the user will then await its completion, signified by a new prompt from the *shell*, before initiating the execution of another process. On a multi-user, multi-process system, this is not an absolute necessity and UNIX provides a facility which allows the user to instruct the *shell* that it is to begin the execution of one process, and then to prompt directly for the next command without waiting for the current process to terminate. To use this facility, the appropriate command line is terminated with the '&' character before the 'return', as in:

```
$ cc -c test.c &
16487
$ ed subs.f
```

Here the first command will set the C compiler on the task of compiling a program, while the second begins an editing session on another file without waiting for the compilation to be completed. (The number echoed by the *shell* is the **process identity** for the process that has just been created by use of the '&' to run in **background** mode.)

There are some limitations to the use of this facility. One is formed by the physical limitations of the cpu power. Starting too many processes at once from a terminal (or several terminals) will simply overload the cpu, and the throughput of the system will be reduced due to excess swapping of processes in and out of the main memory. Many of the tasks that we normally perform on a computer are also essentially sequential in nature, and even where concurrent execution of processes can be used effectively, the nature of the terminal handler makes it virtually impossible for more than one of these to interact in any way with the terminal. To ensure that this does not become a problem, any processes run using the '&' facility are executed in background mode; this chiefly differs from the normal running mode in that the standard input is defaulted to a null file, rather than to the user's keyboard.

To determine the state of any processes that may have been set running in this manner, we can use the utility program *ps*. (Normally there is no indication of the termination of processes, other than any messages that the processes themselves may be set to output for this purpose.) *ps* reports on the **status** of all of the currently running processes that have been initiated from our terminal—the presence of a process on the list printed out indicates that this process is still active, while its absence from the list shows that it has completed. (The *shell* will always be present in the list, of course, under its system name of 'sh'). Additional information is provided for each process, including the unique process identity number that is allocated to each process by the scheduler.

14.2.1   Synchronisation of processes

UNIX V7 provides no particular mechanism for synchronising one process with another, or for passing messages and signals between processes, apart from the forms to be described in Section 14.3, but they apply to only a limited class of cases: essentially where one process has initiated the execution of another.

Processes that are created by executing shell programs can perform a rather 'string and sealing wax' form of synchronisation by using the 'while' and 'until' constructs which allow a program to suspend on a particular condition. In this case, the particular condition can be for one process (the receiver) to use *test* to determine whether or not a given file exists, and to suspend execution until it does. The other process, (the transmitter) signals to the receiver by creating the appropriate file (which may be empty). If required, messages may also be passed in the file.

The following group of *shell* statements shows how this might be organised in the receiver process, with the appropriate file being generated in the transmitter process.

The use of *sleep* ensures that processing time is not wasted unduly, and the parameter of this can be selected according to the response required.

```
: a sample of shell program code to wait for a
: file to be created by another process before
: proceeding
until test -f <filename>
do
      sleep 30
done
```

The above method is not particularly elegant when compared with the inter-task communication facilities to be found in many other operating systems—but then we are not necessarily going to require such a facility very often. While some problems are solved well by running several processes concurrently, they are not particularly common problems, nor is this form of solution one that is immediately attractive to every programmer.

When running more than one process from a terminal, another useful utility program is the *wait* process. When run, this will suspend itself until all of the processes previously started by the user via the '&' facility have terminated, and will report if any have terminated abnormally. Using an option of this process, it can also be set to await the termination of one particular process. *wait* is intended primarily for use in writing shell programs, and provides the *shell* with a form of **exception handling** for the case where a process terminates on an error.

Another facility that may come in useful when running concurrent processes is *tee*. As might be expected from the name, this process is particularly intended for use with pipes, and its task is to make a copy of its standard input to both its standard output as well as to another file, specified as a parameter. So a sequence such as:

```
$ proc1 | tee copy.dat | proc2
```

will copy the standard output of 'proc1' to the standard input of 'proc2', while also making a copy in the file 'copy.dat' on the way. Again, this facility is primarily useful for writing shell programs.

14.2.2   The scheduling of processes on UNIX

The scheduling scheme used by UNIX is a fairly simple one. At any time all of the current processes (i.e. those that are currently being executed) possess a priority, and for all active processes, the processor will execute the process with the highest priority. A process becomes 'not active' when it is suspended to await any form of resource (including inputs).

The current processes are further divided into two groups. **System processes** are those that are closely tied to the running of the operating system, such as device driver processes and of course the *shell*. **User processes** are those that are run by users from their terminals, including the system utility programs. System processes are given high priority values, while user processes are given a lower priority value in order to ensure that the actions that are important for the efficient functioning of the Operating System are performed quickly. If any system process is active, then the scheduler will always choose to run this in preference to any user processes available.

Among themselves the user processes are also scheduled on a 'round robin' basis. Each process in turn gets a slice of the cpu time, with the size of the slice being adjusted so that those processes that make heavy use of the cpu and perform little input/output get rather less frequent opportunities to be executed than those that often fail to use up their whole timeslice. The latter are usually processes that are performing a lot of input/output, being suspended frequently to await further data or to complete their output sequence. The scheme used to adjust the size of the timeslice is adaptive, so that a process is scheduled according to its current behaviour at any point during its execution.

A significant point that arises from this is that UNIX is not in any sense a **real-time** operating system. It is designed to serve the needs of a community of cooperating users for program development and use—not directly to service laboratory instruments or to perform process control functions. Where such needs exist, they may need to be met by other means such as using a satellite processor as a buffer in order to provide the necessary real-time response rates.

14.3   Process creation and execution

In order to be able to schedule processes and to determine their resource needs, the operating system maintains a table which contains all of the relevant information about the current processes; this is known as the **process table**. A process will acquire an entry in this table when the *shell* is requested to run the process, and the entry is removed when the process terminates. While a process is actually resident in the main memory and is active, there will also be a **system data** block of memory which is associated with it and which is used to hold information needed by the system in order to support requests from the process. This block cannot be accessed directly by the process itself. Whenever the process is not active, for example because it has been swapped out of main memory, the information required to resume the process when it returns to main memory will be held in the process table.

The creation of a new process is not performed by simply copying the contents of an executable program file into main memory, but rather it depends upon the use of a mechanism known as the **fork**, used together with the **exec** facility. These are described a little more fully in section 14.3.1.

14.3.1   **fork** and **exec**

fork is a system primitive (i.e. a very low-level procedure), and when a process calls to the executive of the operating system to perform a fork, the effect will be for it to make a copy of that process in main memory. This is a full copy of the original process, and any files that were open before the call to fork will now be open for both the original (parent) process and the new (child) process. Each version of the process is informed whether it is the child or the parent process via the return value from the fork function: if it is the child then a value of zero is returned; for the parent, the value returned is the process identity of the child process just created.

After a fork, this return value may be used as the condition for an 'if-then-else' construct, so that the parent and child processes can execute different sequences. A common form is for the parent process to suspend itself and wait for the child process to terminate, while the child process proceeds to perform the appropriate actions. An example of such a use of the fork for a program written in C might be as follows.

```
if ( fork()==0 )
{
    sequence of actions for the child process
}
else
    { sequence of actions for the parent process }
```

This feature becomes particularly significant when the child process then uses a form of the **exec** primitive. If the child process uses exec with an executable file as one of the arguments, then the code and data from the file will be copied down to replace the code and data segments of the child process in memory. It remains the same process in terms of its process identity and its relationship with the parent process—but it will now execute using a different program.

The fork and exec mechanisms together provide a means by which one process may organise the execution of another. The sequence for this is as follows.

(1) The code of the process calls the fork primitive.
(2) The next part of the code (executed by both parent and child) then tests to see which of these it is. Using the 'if-then-else' form, one clause (for the parent) directs it either to exit or to wait the termination of the child process, while the other clause (for the child) directs it to exec the appropriate file containing the new program to be executed.
(3) The child process now executes the new program until termination, upon which the parent process may resume if appropriate.

Figure 14.1 shows this sequence of actions in diagrammatic form.

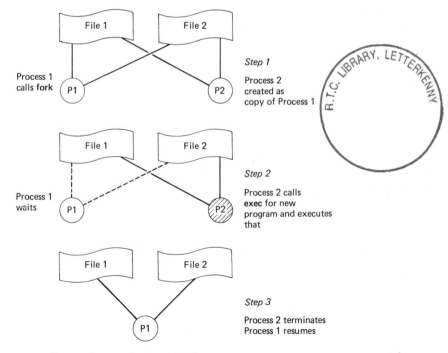

Fig. 14.1 Process creation and execution on UNIX

This sequence provides a limited means of synchronising two processes, and it is also the mechanism by which the *shell* is able to execute our commands by acting as the parent process. So when we give a command such as

```
$ ls
```

the *shell* will make a copy of itself, and the child version will then exec the file containing the binary image of *ls*. Since this will have full information about any files that are open at the call to exec, we can now see how such features as the redirection of standard input and standard output can be very easily organised by the *shell*, simply by opening the appropriate files before performing the fork.

15

Device driver processes

15.1 Introduction

This short final chapter is really specific to the PDP-11 family of computers, although the general points are relevant to any machine that directly handles its own input and output. Since many machines designed after the PDP-11, such as the VAX11 and the Motorola MC68000, have designs that were very heavily influenced by that of the PDP-11, this chapter contains material that is likely to be relevant to these too. It is assumed that the reader has some familiarity with the general structure of the PDP-11 computers.

15.2 Devices on the PDP-11

The PDP-11 is a member of that class of machines that have no special instructions to control input from, and output to, devices. Instead it uses a principle known as the **external page** so that input and output can be performed along a single data highway, or bus. The bus is also used for accessing the main memory, and so input and output can be performed using the standard memory-accessing machine-level instructions.

In this scheme, any devices available are interfaced to the single bus of the computer via an **interface**. This item of hardware performs the task of bridging the gap between the forms of signal used by the computer, along the bus, and the forms of signal used by the device. Apart from converting between different voltage levels and communication conventions, this may also involve converting between parallel and serial forms of data transmission.

By convention, the device interfaces are set to respond to a memory access cycle which uses a memory address within the top **page** of the memory address range (hence the term **external page**). In the case of the PDP-11, this is an address within the top 4K words of memory, and on a machine without virtual addressing hardware, this leaves only 28K words of address space for use by programs and data. 'Simple' devices such as line printers and terminals are each accessed by a pair of registers, which occupy predetermined positions in the 4K address space. Usually one register is concerned with the tasks of device control and status reporting, while the other provides a buffer for reading or writing the actual data. More complex devices, often using direct memory access techniques, will utilise much larger numbers of registers within the address space.

Because these device registers appear to the cpu to be ordinary memory locations on the bus, and are hence accessible to the normal data manipulation instructions from the machine's instruction set, it is possible to write the device driver programs in a high level language such as C. Even for a system such as UNIX, where the virtual memory segmentation hardware may also need to be manipulated by a device driver in order to access a user's buffers, this still holds good since the virtual memory descriptor and address registers are themselves positioned in the external page.

Chapter 13 described how file access is organised on the UNIX system, and how devices are accessed via special files. The protocols for such accesses have been standardised in UNIX V7, and therefore the task of adding a new device driver, or of writing one, is much easier than on previous versions. Essentially the device driver consists of a set of related procedures, performing a basic set of device-related functions and with the different forms of file access primitives being mapped to the appropriate procedure for a given device.

15.3   Changing device drivers and adding new ones

Since UNIX V7 is issued in source form, the source code for all of the device drivers considered standard to UNIX is also a part of the issue. (Even with the look-alikes and re-worked versions of UNIX that are normally supplied only in binary form, it is not unusual to find that source files are provided for the device drivers.) It is therefore possible for an experienced programmer to modify a device driver. The only requirements are to understand how the device works, and to be able to read C! On the whole such changes are only rarely required, and when they are required then they are usually needed to accommodate a new variant of device, perhaps by adding support for some features that it may possess.

The UNIX system is issued with a range of device drivers that can be used with most of the commonly encountered devices. (Information about the characteristics of the device drivers provided as a part of the UNIX operating system is given in Section 4 of the UNIX manual.) When the system is configured for a particular installation, the details of available devices and their minor devices are included within the instructions to the construction software. In particular, the *mkconf* utility program takes a file containing a list of the devices present and produces the routines needed to initialise the appropriate interrupt vectors and to set up the system tables. Of course, the device driver programs must also be present in the directory /dev.

The two key files that are involved when adding new devices, or reconfiguring existing ones, are 'l.s' and 'c.c'. The first of these is an assembler source file used to construct the initialisation code for the operating system; this connects the device driver to the interrupt vectors so that the correct device driver code is used to handle device requests. The second file, 'c.c', is used to map the user's file handling calls to the appropriate routines within the device driver itself, e.g. 'open', 'read', write', etc.

Adding new devices and, in some cases, adding more of the same device, thus requires a rebuild of the operating system, in order to include the appropriate tables and to incorporate the set of procedures that make up the device driver. Since most of the work involved is performed by *make*, this represents a fairly straightforward task of maintenance for the system programmer.

15.4   Writing device driver programs

This section is not intended to be any form of step-by-step guide for the system programmer through all of the problems likely to be encountered in writing a device driver program. Rather it tries to make a few points about the technique and about the problems commonly found when handling device interfaces on a PDP-11.

In taking on the task of writing a device driver program, a programmer needs to be:

(i)   familiar with the form that PDP-11 input and output takes, and with the characteristics of the particular device involved;

(ii)   conversant with the UNIX protocols for input and output.

The form of PDP-11 input and output is well documented in the DEC literature, and the UNIX form for protocols used in interfacing user processes to device drivers is likewise documented. However, in reading about either of these it is helpful to have a listing of a suitable UNIX device driver to hand in order to see from an example how these things can be handled in C. For example, if the task is to write a driver for a pen plotter device, then a suitably similar device would be the paper tape punch. Using the listing for this device, one can then identify

(a)   the device-related parts of the code;
(b)   system-interface parts of the code.

It is thus possible to learn about the UNIX style of driver construction.

(A word of warning. Despite its apparent simplicity as a device, the terminal is not a simple example to consider. One reason is that a terminal is treated as being two distinct devices, using two pairs of interface registers. Another is that the terminal handler normally contains a lot of extra code to handle the various control key options such as 'delete' etc.)

The 'simple' devices that are wholly program controlled are usually easier to handle as a first attempt. While the more simple of the Direct Memory Access (DMA) interfaces are not too demanding to program, there are some messy items in setting up the eighteen bit addressing of the PDP-11 bus, since this involves the use of a sixteen bit register plus two bits in another register!

Various system primitives are provided for use within a device driver, including primitives to fetch a character from a user's buffer and to output to a user's buffer—so avoiding a need to handle the segmentation hardware directly. Primitives are also available for such functions as synchronisation of parts of a driver, and a 'timeout' facility, which is useful where we need to be able to escape if the device is inactive and does not respond with an interrupt.

Once complete, the special file for the new device driver will need to be copied to the directory /dev, and the appropriate information inserted into the input file used by *mkconf*. If a device is a non-standard one, then the system will have no built-in knowledge of its characteristics and such information as vector addresses and type (character or block) will also need to be supplied.

Writing and debugging device drivers is not a particularly simple task on a running system, since being privileged programs in a number of ways, any errors are apt to corrupt the operating system within the machine—with obvious results. However, UNIX does make life relatively easy by providing the C language and a well-defined interface. After that it is left for the programmer to understand how the device is to be used and controlled.

References

Two documents from the UNIX manual that are particularly relevant are as follows.

1. Thompson, K, *UNIX Implementation*, UNIX V7.
2. Ritchie, D M, *The UNIX I/O System*, UNIX V7.

Special characters

Index